Johanna Thiel

Boxers

Everything About Housing, Care,
Nutrition, Breeding, and Health Care

Filled with Full-color Photographs
Illustrations by Renate Holzner

BARRON'S

2 CONTENTS

THE TYPICAL BOXER

Breed Characteristics

"If the Boxer didn't exist, we would have to invent one!" What other dog can make such wrinkles appear upon its forehead? What other dog can look at you so faithfully that you simply can't be angry at it? Often Boxers are called the philosophers of the dog world. That may be attributable to the fact that they frequently seem somewhat dreamy and absentminded, yet the next instant they can be fully alert and ready to protect their family from anything.

The character of a dog is made up of instincts and hereditary factors, with all the modifications brought about by environmental influences. Typical of the Boxer's nature, and definitely its most prominent feature, is the juxtaposition of a number of very different sets of traits. These traits, however, coexist in complete harmony: On the one hand, the Boxer exhibits fearlessness and unflinching courage; it is self-assured and possesses high spirits and energy in equal measure, and its alertness is legendary. On the other hand, it also is characterized by pronounced affection and loyalty where its significant human and all other family members are concerned. Its special characteristics also include its playfulness, which persists well into old age. Moreover, it loves children and cannot be bribed by strangers. All these qualities make the Boxer easy to keep as a pet,

The typical Boxer has an intimidating face but an extremely warm heart.

despite its size, and an ideal dog for a family. If opposite characteristics are displayed, they are faults of that particular Boxer, and they must be interpreted as defects in that dog's character.

Because of its pronounced liveliness and desire for activity, the Boxer needs a great deal of attention and involvement on the part of its owner.

Origin of the Breed

Boxers have a long history that goes back to ancient times. From his Indian campaign, Alexander the Great brought home huge dogs of the old Mastiff type whose distinguishing feature was their wide mouth. By contrast, the other dogs of antiquity had pointed mouths. The dogs brought back by Alexander probably formed the initial basis for the breeding of Molossian Hounds. This breed's name came from its origin in the Greek province in which the Molossian royal family ruled. Later, dogs of such origin also came into use by the Romans. They were considered invincible until the "Britannic Mastiffs," huge British fighting dogs, appeared on the scene. They had an even broader mouth and even greater strength than the Molossian dogs, and for that reason they gradually replaced the Molossians. From then on the two breeds were crossed with each other, though their offspring continued to bear the name of Molossian Hounds. These dogs are one ancestral line of our present-day Boxer.

The second line is represented by the Mastiffs, which were bred from the British fighting dogs. Their appearance, size, and body weight varied, depending on the purpose for which they were used.

The third line developed among the Celts and Germanic tribes. They too bred large dogs that were unusually rugged and powerful. Central Europe produced the large, or Danzig, "bullenbeisser" (bull biter) and the small, or Brabant, bullenbeisser. This lighter bullenbeisser is considered the immediate ancestor of today's Boxers.

The Direct Ancestors

In those days the breeding of the bullenbeisser was mostly under the control of hunters who performed their services exclusively for ruling houses. It was the bullenbeisser's job to seize the game driven by the tracking Hounds and hang onto the animal until the hunter came and killed his quarry. For this task, the dog needed as wide a mouth as possible, with a broad bite. Only thus equipped could it get

a firm grip with its teeth and then hold tightly to its quarry. Through breeding, the upper jaw became progressively shortened. The result was the protrusive occlusion that allowed the dog enough room to breathe while holding on to the quarry. This overbite is typical of the Boxer.

Efforts to Improve the Breed

Breeding of pedigreed Boxers did not begin in Germany until the second half of the eighteenth century. The bullenbeisser of the eighteenth century did not yet represent a uniform type. Many of them were mongrels or were crossed with bulldogs. Nonetheless, there was a centuries-long tradition of linebreeding with the bullenbeisser. That made it possible to work on developing a uniform type. The name "Boxer" for this uniform type first made its appearance between 1860 and 1870. A little later, in 1895, some proponents of linebreeding of Boxers joined together to found a Boxer club in Munich. It was they who also made the Munich "beer Boxer" of their day into the popular family pet and utility dog known today. Today it is very hard to imagine how difficult that was to accomplish, in the absence of any knowledge of genetics and of bloodlines.

Another of the achievements of the newly founded Boxer club was the authoritative establishment of the breed standard. Previously, breeding had been based solely on a practical point of view: Matings took place in accordance with the intended use. Now there existed a guideline independent of that practice, a guideline to which breeders as well as judges could adhere.

A brindle male Boxer, as specified in the breed standard.

One of the first Boxer kennels to make a name for itself with its breeding program was vom Dom. The owner, Friderun Stockmann, thus laid the basis for a Boxer strain that was highly respected in Germany and elsewhere. From it came the legendary Lustig vom Dom. Many of today's Boxers are descended from that stud.

The first United States Boxer was registered in 1904. An import, the famous Sieger Dampf von Dom became the first United States champion in 1915. This dog was owned by Herbert H. Lehman, who later became the governor of New York State. Popularity of the breed skyrocketed when Ch. Warlord of Mazelaine won best in show at the 1947 Westminster Kennel Club competition.

The AKC Breed Standard

The standard for a dog breed describes in ideal terms all the features a representative of that breed should possess. The specifications of the breed standard, which are obligatory, are always laid down in a studbook. They must be adhered to in breeding. At the same time, these guidelines serve the judges at dog shows as a basis for their scoring.

The studbook also contains a record of all the breeding particulars. Thus it supplies the family tree for the entire breed, and for each puppy from a breeding program it is possible to call up the entire gallery of its forebears. The studbook is, so to speak, a marriage license register for dogs.

General Appearance

The ideal Boxer is a medium-sized, square-built dog of good substance with a short back, strong limbs, and short, tight-fitting coat. Its well-developed muscles are clean, hard, and appear smooth under taut skin. Its movements denote energy. The gait is firm, yet elastic, the stride free and ground-covering, the carriage proud. Developed to serve as guard, working, and companion dog, the Boxer combines strength and agility with elegance and style. Its expression is alert and temperament steadfast and tractable. The chiseled head imparts to the Boxer a unique individual stamp. It must be in correct proportion to the body. The broad, blunt muzzle is the distinctive feature, and great value is placed upon its being of proper form and balance with the skull. In judging the Boxer, first consideration is given to general appearance to which attractive color and arresting style contribute. Next is overall balance with special attention devoted to the head, after which the individual body components are examined for their correct construction, and the efficiency of gait is evaluated.

Height, Proportion, Substance

Height: Adult males 22.5 to 25 inches (57–63.5 cm); females 21 to 23.5 inches (53–59.7 cm) at the withers. Preferably, males should not be under the minimum nor females over the maximum: however, proper balance and quality in the individual should be of primary importance because there is no size disqualification.

Proportion: The body in profile is of square proportion in that a horizontal line from the front of the forechest to the rear projection of the upper thigh should equal the length of a vertical line dropped from the top of the withers to the ground.

Substance: Sturdy with balanced musculature. Males larger boned than their female counterparts.

Head

The beauty of the head depends upon harmonious proportion of muzzle to skull. The blunt muzzle is one third the length of the head from the occiput to the tip of the nose, and two thirds the width of the skull. The head should be clean, not showing deep wrinkles (wet). Wrinkles typically appear upon the forehead when ears are erect, and folds are always present from the lower edge of the stop running downward on both sides of the muzzle.

Expression: Intelligent and alert.

Eyes: Dark brown in color, not too small, too protruding, or too deep-set. Their mood-mirroring character combined with the wrinkling of the forehead, gives the Boxer head its unique quality of expressiveness.

Ears: Set at the highest point of the head, cut rather long and tapering, raised when alert.

All Boxers tend to have very strong legs, but they come in many sizes and colors.

The typical Boxer's coat is short, shiny, and light to the body.

Skull: The top of the skull is slightly arched, not rounded, flat nor noticeably broad, with the occiput not overly pronounced. The forehead shows a slight indentation between the eyes and forms a distinct stop with the topline of the muzzle. The cheeks should be relatively flat and not bulge (cheekiness), maintaining the clean lines of the skull and should taper into the muzzle in a slight, graceful curve.

Muzzle: The muzzle, proportionately developed in length, width, and depth, has a shape influenced first through the formation of both jawbones, second through the placement of the teeth, and third through the texture of the lips. The top of the muzzle should not slant down (downfaced), nor should it be concave (dishfaced); however, the tip of the nose should lie slightly higher than the root of the muzzle. The nose should be broad and black. The upper jaw is broad where attached to the skull and maintains this breadth except for a very slight tapering to the front. The lips, which complete the formation of the muzzle, should meet evenly in front. The upper lip is thick and padded, filling out the frontal space created by the projection of the lower jaw, and laterally is supported by the canines of the lower jaw. Therefore, these canines must stand far apart and be of good length so that the front surface of the muzzle is broad and squarish and, when viewed from the side, shows moderate layback. The chin should be perceptible from the side as well as from the front.

Bite: The Boxer bite is undershot; the lower jaw protrudes beyond the upper and curves slightly upward. The incisor teeth of the lower jaw are in a straight line, with the canines preferably up front in the same line to give the jaw the greatest possible width. The upper line of incisors is slightly convex with the corner upper incisors fitting snuggled-in back of the lower canine teeth on each side.

Faults: Skull too broad. Cheekiness. Wrinkling too deep (wet) or lacking (dry). Excessive flews. Muzzle too light for skull. Too pointed a bite (snipy), too undershot, teeth or tongue showing when mouth closed. Eyes noticeably lighter than ground color of coat.

Neck, Topline, Body

Neck: Round, of ample length, muscular and clean without excessive hanging skin (dewlap). The neck has a distinctly marked nape with an elegant arch blending smoothly into the withers.

Topline: Smooth, firm, and slightly sloping.

Body: The chest is of fair width, and the forechest well defined and visible from the side. The brisket is deep, reaching down to the elbows; the depth of the body at the lowest point of the brisket equals half the height of the dog at the withers. The ribs, extending far to the rear, are well-arched but not barrel-shaped. The back is short, straight and muscular and firmly connects the withers to the hindquarters. The loins are short and muscular. The lower line is slightly tucked up, blending into a graceful curve to the rear. The croup is slightly sloped, flat and broad. Tail is set high, docked and carried upward. Pelvis long and in females especially broad.

Faults: Short, heavy neck. Chest too broad, too narrow, or hanging between the shoulders. Lack of forechest. Hanging stomach. Slab-sided rib cage. Long or narrow loin, weak union with croup. Falling off of croup. Higher in rear than in front.

Forequarters

The shoulders are long and sloping, close-lying, and not excessively covered with muscle (loaded). The upper arm is long, approaching a right angle to the shoulder blade. The elbows should not press too closely to the chest wall nor stand off visibly from it. The forelegs are long, straight and firmly muscled and when viewed from the front, stand parallel to each other. The pastern is strong and distinct, slightly slanting, but standing almost perpendicular to the ground. The dewclaws may be removed. Feet should be compact, turning neither in nor out, with well arched toes.

Faults: Loose or loaded shoulders. Tied in or bowed out elbows.

Hindquarters

The hindquarters are strongly muscled with angulation in balance with that of the forequarters. The thighs are broad and curved, the breech musculature hard and strongly developed. Upper and lower thigh long. Leg well-angulated at the stifle with a clearly defined, well "let down" hock joint. Viewed from behind, the hind legs should be straight with hock joints leaning neither in nor out. From the side, the leg below the hock (metatarsus) should be almost perpendicular to the ground, with a slight slope to the rear permissible. The metatarsus should be short, clean, and strong. The Boxer has no rear dewclaws.

Faults: Steep or over-angulated hindquarters. Light thighs or overdeveloped hams. Over-angulated (sickle) hocks. Hindquarters too far under or too far behind.

Coat

Short, shiny, lying smooth and tight to the body.

Color

The colors are fawn and brindle. Fawn shades vary from light tan to mahogany. The brindle ranges from sparse, but clearly defined black stripes on a fawn background, to such a heavy concentration of black striping that the essential fawn background color barely, although clearly, shows through (which may create the appearance of "reverse brindling"). White markings should be of such distribution as to enhance the dog's appearance, but may not exceed one-third of the entire coat. They are not desirable on the flanks or on the back of the torso proper. On the face, white may replace part of the otherwise essential black

Left, a Boxer with a normal stance, viewed from the rear. The dog in the center has bandy legs; the Boxer on the right is cow-hocked.

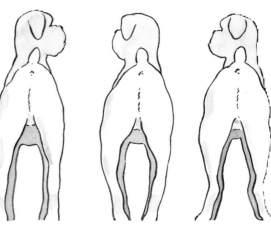

mask and may extend in an upward path between the eyes, but it must not be excessive, so as to detract from true Boxer expression.

Faults: Unattractive or misplaced white markings.

Disqualifications: Boxers that are any color other than fawn or brindle. Boxers with a total of white markings exceeding one-third of the entire coat.

Gait

Viewed from the side, proper front and rear angulation is manifested in a smoothly efficient level-backed, ground covering stride with powerful drive emanating from a freely operating rear. Although the front legs do not contribute impelling power, adequate "reach" should be evident to prevent interference, overlap or "sidewinding" (crabbing). Viewed from the front, the shoulders should remain trim and the elbows not flare out. The legs are parallel until gaiting narrows the track in proportion to increasing speed, then the legs come in under the body but should never cross. The line from the shoulder down through the leg should remain straight although not necessarily perpendicular to the ground. Viewed from the rear, a Boxer's rump should not roll. The hind feet should "dig in" and track relatively true with the front. Again, as speed increases, the normally broad rear track will become narrower.

Faults: Stilted or inefficient gait. Lack of smoothness.

Character and Temperament

These are of paramount importance in the Boxer. Instinctively a "hearing" guard dog, his bearing is alert, dignified, and self-assured. In the show ring, his behavior should exhibit constrained animation. With family and friends, his temperament is fundamentally playful, yet patient and stoical with children. Deliberate and wary with strangers, he will exhibit curiosity but, most importantly, fearless courage if threatened. However, he responds promptly to friendly overtures honestly rendered. His intelligence, loyal affection, and tractability to discipline make him a highly desirable companion.

Faults: Lack of dignity and alertness. Shyness.

The preceding description is that of the ideal Boxer. Any deviations from the above described dog must be penalized to the extent of the deviation.

When you buy a Boxer you are assuming a great responsibility, because the dog is totally at the mercy of its owner. Before you decide to purchase a Boxer, therefore, you need to think about a few things:

✔ A Boxer's life expectancy is about 10 to 12 years. Can you guarantee that your pet will be well cared for in your household for that length of time?

✔ Do your living conditions meet the requirements of such an animal? Not everyone who decides to buy a Boxer has to have a house with a yard—although that would be ideal. Boxers also can be kept very easily in an apartment or condo (if exercised daily), because they are quiet dogs. However, the apartment should not be small, because Boxers have a great need for activity and require a corresponding degree of freedom of movement.

✔ To keep a dog in a rented apartment, you need the written agreement of the landlord, in advance.

✔ The issue of "going outdoors" is particularly important where a rented apartment is concerned. Is there a vacant area in the immediate vicinity where the Boxer can relieve itself? If there is not, you may possibly have to drive several miles to find a suitable spot.

✔ Who will look after your Boxer when you go on vacation? Do you have in mind destinations to which your dog could easily accompany you?

Licenses and Insurance

If you have made the decision to buy a Boxer, you have to keep the following in mind as well:

✔ In most areas, buying a dog license is one of the duties of the dog owner.

✔ License applications can be obtained by calling or writing your city or municipality and requesting an application. In addition, most veterinarians have license forms available at their office.

✔ Double check your homeowners insurance policy to make certain you are adequately covered under your policy's liability clause in the event your dog does damage to person or property. If needed, add or increase your coverage to give you that all-important peace of mind.

✔ Health insurance for dogs is also available now (see Information, page 92). Each dog owner must decide individually whether taking out such a policy is advisable.

A Male or a Female?

The question of whether it is more convenient to get a male or a female cannot be answered in a clear-cut way. The gender of your pet—just like its color—is primarily a matter of personal preference. Nonetheless, there

There are many things you should know before deciding to share your home with a Boxer, such as this gentle giant.

The puppy licks the mother dog's chops to show that it wants to be fed.

A Puppy or an Adult Dog?

This decision is a matter of personal preference. However, purchasing a puppy will allow you to have some control over its training. If the dog later develops peculiarities nonetheless, then at least they are your responsibility. When buying an adult dog, you need to find out the precise reasons that led the previous owners to sell their pet. In this way you are better prepared for potential surprises such as inability to get along with other dogs or other peculiarities.

Living with other animals: How well the newly acquired Boxer is able to share a household with other pets depends on its age. Certainly a puppy will come to terms with other animals more easily than an adult dog, which may already have had negative experiences. In such cases you need to make sure that each animal acknowledges the other's living space.

One Dog or Two?

A single Boxer feels very comfortable as the "supreme ruler" in the family. Its playmates are, by and large, the members of the family. It even prefers them to another dog that is not part of the family. If you want to add a second Boxer to your household, keep the following in mind:

✔ You will have twice the amount of work when it comes to feeding and grooming the dogs.

✔ Please remember that every dog, whether a loner or part of a pack, is an individual

are some objective reasons as well that may decide the issue in favor of a certain gender:

A male will be larger, heavier, and stronger than a female. A Boxer 25 inches (63.5 cm) high at the withers can reach the considerable weight of about 71 pounds (32 kg). Its size and strength are factors to consider. A fully grown male Boxer, because of its boisterous response to other males, can be physically very exhausting for its owner. Here, so-called dominance behavior plays a major role. On the other hand, a male naturally will not bring any unplanned offspring home, even if it has managed to run off despite careful supervision.

A female, as a rule, is smaller and lighter than a male. She also is usually somewhat more alert; after all, as a mother she has to rear her puppies. However, a female normally is in season twice a year. Many people wish to avoid the minor inconveniences associated with this so-called heat (see The Mating Act, page 85). Suppressing estrus with medications, however, is not advisable. Such treatments often result in subsequent impairment of the dog's health, such as inflammation of the uterus.

with particular character traits and its own temperament.

✔ When choosing a vacation site, you need to know whether you can take along the second dog, too.

A second Boxer: If a second Boxer joins your household, your first pet needs a few days to get used to the new dog. If your pet is already fairly advanced in years, a surprise is in store for you: The Boxer will be rejuvenated.

The fewest problems in adjustment will arise if the new addition and your present Boxer form a male-female pair. In any event, the adjustment process is substantially easier for a puppy if there is already another dog in the family.

In a Household with Children

As a family dog, a Boxer poses no difficulty in its dealings with children. It is irrelevant whether you have a male or a female. The children need to learn, however, not to treat their Boxer as they would a toy or to hurt it. When dealing with puppies in particular, you need to be careful, because puppies are definitely capable of inflicting painful bites and scratches. Always keep an eye on small children when your Boxer is present. Then you can intervene at once if the Boxer's liveliness ever gives rise to a dangerous situation.

What the Buyer Needs to Know

Once you have decided that a Boxer is right for you, the next question, of course, is this: "Where do I get a Boxer?" It is best to buy a puppy from a breeder who belongs to the American Boxer Club or from a pet store that obtains its Boxers from such a breeder (see Information, page 92).

How to Find a Good Breeder

Addresses of reliable Boxer breeders are also obtainable from the American Kennel Club (AKC) (see Information on page 92). The AKC also has an excellent video about Boxers. This videotape would probably be a very good investment for any potential Boxer owner.

There are specialized magazines and newsletters available that deal with Boxers

---

TIP

Signs of a Healthy Puppy
✔ The puppy has a thick coat of hair with a silky gloss. It should not be dull and lusterless.
✔ Its eyes are clear and bright. They should not be dull or tearing.

In addition, a normally developed, healthy puppy is always:
✔ *curious:* It will explore its surroundings thoroughly and approach humans with interest. The puppy should not be fearful.
✔ *lively:* The puppy is active, moves nimbly, and reacts to all external stimuli. It should not be apathetic.
✔ *playful:* The puppy accepts every invitation to play and makes appropriate use of every object offered for play.

Curiosity, but not fearfulness, is a sign of a healthy Boxer pup.

This beach bum looks ready for a swim.

(ask your local dog club about these publications). The Internet can also provide you with a wealth of information. By learning as much as you can about Boxer breeders, you will be in a better position to choose the place to obtain your Boxer.

Other places to contact:

✔ In many areas you may find Boxer clubs. Talk with the members and get their recommendations of possible sources. There may be a Boxer breeders' organization in your city or state. Boxer breeders/exhibitors generally know who among their peers has a litter of pups, an older pet-quality puppy, or an adult Boxer in need of a good home. Because these are the

people who show dogs, they probably can help you find a pup with dog show potential. Often these Boxer clubs have appropriate training sites.

✔ When you see a Boxer owner on the street, don't hesitate to ask him or her about the dog's origin. As a rule, owners are glad to give you the address of their pet's breeder.

Note: It is not a good idea to get a Boxer through a puppy mill or mail-order business. In these transactions, the dog is ordered and delivered as freight. Thus, you have no idea in advance how your dog looks or what its parentage is. Consequently, you also receive no pedigree.

How to Choose a Puppy

In choosing a puppy, let your personal taste guide your decision. You have ample time available to make your selection, because a puppy should never go to a new home before its eighth week of life. Until that time you can keep coming back to look over the litter. Naturally it is best if you pick a likely candidate early on. Then you can keep visiting it to play with it. In this way it will have a chance to grow accustomed to you.

In addition to its state of health (see Signs of a Healthy Puppy, on page 15), the puppy's temperament should be an important criterion in making your choice. After all, you would like a dog that suits you and your style of life. Pay close attention to the individual "personalities" in the litter. If you want a lively housemate, pick a puppy that romps boisterously with its littermates and also comes up to you immediately when you visit. If a calmer type is more apt to appeal to your temperament, then the right puppy for you is the one that is not involved in every tussle and sometimes watches the goings-on with interest from the sidelines. In any event, however, your ideal puppy should be bright and responsive. Don't let yourself be guided by pity to choose a puppy that is poorly socialized. A proper Boxer will always be a bundle of energy. Caution is in order if there is any indication of illness or behavioral disturbance.

Most puppies, regardless of breed, tend to have voracious appetites.

Advantages of Buying from a Professional Breeder or Reputable Pet Retailer

A reputable seller of Boxers voluntarily adheres to the American Boxer Club's regulations governing purebred dogs and their health. If you buy your Boxer from such a source, you will not only be getting an animal that conforms to the breed standard; you also will have the guarantee that the puppy has had the best possible care:

✔ At the breeder's, the puppies grow up together as a litter, and the imprinting phase, which begins after the third week (see Developmental Phases, page 41), in most cases is characterized by human contact and loving rearing.

✔ With a dog from a reputable source, moreover, you have the assurance that it has been well nourished. Because reputable sellers usually take a systematic approach to nutrition, they are also able to document precisely what the puppy has been fed.

Tip: At first, feed your puppy exactly what the seller gave it. Switching to a different food is very difficult for the puppy. If the switch is made too soon, painful gastrointestinal upsets can result. For this reason, have the seller give you a feeding plan.

Vaccination Certificate and Worming

You have two additional advantages when you buy your Boxer from a reputable source:

✔ The puppy has received its preliminary vaccinations against the common canine diseases, such as distemper and parvovirus (see Vaccination Schedule, page 70). The seller has this basic series of immunizations performed within the puppy's first eight weeks of life. The seller should present the buyer with the appropriate proofs of vaccination.

✔ A reputable Boxer seller also makes sure that the puppies are adequately wormed (see Worming, page 69) before they are released to the buyer.

Note: When buying a Boxer, therefore, make absolutely sure that you receive the current health records, showing the dates of all vaccinations, worming, and examinations by a licensed veterinarian, including the results and treatments.

Tail Docking and Ear Cropping

The breed standard of the Boxer requires that its tail be docked. Tail docking is normally performed within the first week of a puppy's life, so that new puppy you purchase should

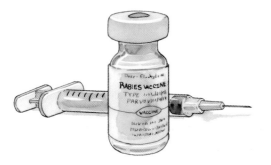

When buying a Boxer, be sure to ask for documentation of its vaccinations.

CHECKLIST

Basic Equipment for Your Boxer

✔ **Collar with leash:** Be sure the new collar is not too tight. Ask your dog's breeder to measure the puppy's neck and tell you what size to buy.

In addition, you need a leash, or lead, about 6.5 feet (2 m) long and not overly heavy. If roughly one third of the leash's lower portion consists of metal links, it is unsuitable, because puppies try to free themselves from this as yet unfamiliar device by biting on the metal links, and damage their teeth. Also unsuitable are dog leashes that retract automatically. Even a young puppy needs to learn a bit of leash discipline, and this type of leash is not appropriate for such lessons.

When the dog is older, it will need a leather leash that can stand up to its high spirits, and a chain-link choke collar, which tightens when the Boxer jerks at its leash.

✔ **Dog bed:** Your puppy's bed is very important to its sense of well-being. Place the bed in a quiet, draft-free spot where the dog will be undisturbed but will not lack contact with its family. In addition, the spot you choose should be kept at a fairly consistent environmental temperature. The dog bed itself should not be overly soft.

✔ **Food dish:** You also need a food bowl and a water bowl. Both should be easy to clean. Pet stores sell models that are difficult to overturn and have adjustable heights. Choose a height setting that suits your dog's size, and move the bowls higher as the Boxer grows. The advantage of these adjustable devices is that they keep your Boxer's forelegs from turning out and becoming bent.

✔ **Toys:** Playthings not only entertain the Boxer and provide playful activity, but also keep it from getting interested in furniture and carpets. Good choices are a hard ball or a solid rubber ring. The ball has to be big enough not to be swallowed by the Boxer. Small rubber toys are not appropriate, because the young dog will gnaw on them and might swallow pieces of them.

Puppies need to satisfy their chewing urge, so purchase sturdy nylon toys that will keep your puppy from teething on your bedroom slippers. These toys have the added benefit of messaging the gums and, consequently, will make the pup feel good, too.

The right way to put on the choke collar: The movable part of the chain should face toward the hand controlling the leash.

*It doesn't matter which look you prefer—
all Boxers tend to make great pets!*

have an artificially shortened tail. At the same time that the tail is docked, the front dewclaws are often removed as well. This is a good idea, since these digital remnants, if left intact, can become easily snagged on carpet and other material, causing painful injuries.

Breed standard also dictates that your Boxer's ears be cropped. Realize, however, that this needs only to be done if you plan on competing your Boxer in AKC-sanctioned events and don't want your dog penalized for having uncropped ears. Otherwise, you may choose to forego this procedure altogether. Most veterinarians prefer performing ear crops between 12 and 16 weeks of age. Cropped ears must be bandaged properly after the procedure to ensure that they stand properly erect. In some instances, ears may need to remain bandaged for several months in order to achieve the desired carriage. Realize that many veterinarians do not crop ears anymore. As a result, it is important to find one who has experience with cropping Boxer ears. Ask fellow Boxer owners or breed club affiliates

for their recommendations. Or better yet, consider saving yourself time and money (and sometimes much grief!) by purchasing a Boxer puppy with it ears already cropped.

Sales Contract

Buying a Boxer is a matter of confidence. Nevertheless, it is advisable to conclude a contract of sale. Appropriate blank contracts are available from the American Boxer Club as well as from the AKC. Such an agreement is not a requirement, but it does offer both the buyer and the breeder a certain degree of protection.

Pedigree

If you have bought your Boxer from a breeder who belongs to the American Boxer Club, you will also receive a pedigree. It is issued by the AKC or the American Boxer Club, because it is the recognized breeders' organization for the Boxer. In the proof of descent issued by the club, the animal's name and origin are recorded. The document also certifies that your dog comes from a supervised breeding program of the American Boxer Club and complies with the breed standard as well as the club's breeding regulations (see The AKC Breed Standard, page 7).

Keep in mind that AKC registration and a long pedigree are no guarantees of quality.

In the role of guard, the Boxer is completely in its element.

When purchasing a Boxer, your best assurance that you are getting a healthy, quality pet is to utilize only reputable breeders or retailers when doing so. In addition, always insist on a prepurchase examination, to be performed by a veterinarian of your choosing, prior to the transfer of any money.

Sources of Danger in Your Home

Naturally your house or apartment contains a number of potential dangers for your puppy. Eliminate these sources of danger before your new pet joins your household.

Cords: Particularly dangerous are all electric cords that are accessible to the Boxer. The dog could chew on them and receive a jolt of current that might prove fatal. You should also keep your telephone cord away from the dog.

Stairs: Slippery or open stairs or, even worse, stairs without railings should not be accessible to the puppy. It could fall.

Dangerous household objects: Put plastic bags, pieces of expanded plastics, and all sharp objects out of reach, because the puppy has a tendency to investigate everything and, if possible, to eat it.

Poisonous substances: Medications, of course, should never be stored where the dog can get at them. The same rule applies to household cleansers as well as to rat and mouse poisons.

Plants: Plants in your house and yard can be poisonous to your little four-legged friend. Someone at your local garden store will be glad to advise you about the plants you already own, and whenever you buy plants in the future, remember to ask about possible danger.

Traveling with Your Pet

For traveling with a young dog, the car is preferable to other modes of transportation, because in a car you will have a chance to stop whenever necessary.

By car: Almost all dogs—including your Boxer—enjoy riding in a car. To test your dog's "road fitness," you can make a short trial run. Before a relatively long car trip, do not feed your dog. It is a good idea to stop every two hours and take a short break to let the dog play and run a little and relieve itself. This is also a good time to give your pet fresh water. Do not feed it until you reach your destination.

Never leave your dog alone in the car in hot weather. Boxers suffer in high temperatures. Your pet might suffer a circulatory collapse that could prove fatal.

Abroad: When you travel abroad, observe the veterinary regulations in force in that country. You can learn what those are by asking your veterinarian or consulting the embassy of the country you plan to visit. In any event, a valid vaccination certificate is a necessity (see page 18). If you plan to take your Boxer aboard an aircraft with you, ask the airline where you can get an approved airline pet carrier. The airlines will be glad to supply you with one for a charge. Have your veterinarian give your Boxer a physical and provide you with a health certificate, which is now a mandatory requirement on all airlines. Be early for all flights and insist on seeing your pet loaded onto the airplane. Discuss the use of canine tranquilizers with your veterinarian and the advisability of your dog making this trip. Very old and very young dogs might be better left at home or in a boarding kennel.

GETTING THE PUPPY SETTLED

Everyone who buys a puppy longs feverishly for the day when the new housemate finally can be picked up and brought home. For the puppy, too, this day is an event of far-reaching significance in its young life: It will be separated from its mother and its littermates. Because it is being wrenched from its familiar environment, it naturally will be feeling very insecure in its new owner's company.

Transporting Your Pet

For the preceding reasons, you should not go alone to pick up your puppy, because it cannot be left unattended, especially in your car. The best time is morning, because the puppy will still have time to gain some familiarity with its new surroundings and family before its first night alone.

Before the trip: Ask the breeder not to give the puppy anything to eat during the hours just before you pick it up. The excitement could cause vomiting and diarrhea in the young puppy.

During the trip: When transporting your puppy, always use a carrier. Line the inside of the carrier with a soft blanket or towel to make it comfortable. In addition, be sure to keep the

It's crucial to make sure your pups always have enough water.

inside of your car cool and well-ventilated. If your puppy cries, resist the temptation to take it out of its carrier. A pup that is transported without a carrier could fall to the floor and become injured if you have to brake suddenly. In addition, as you can imagine, an overactive puppy can pose a real driving hazard.

After the trip and a rest period lasting about one hour, the puppy should be given something to eat. If it is tired then, show it to its daytime sleeping spot. In its designated spot, you can place an old piece of clothing that you have worn, so that it can detect a familiar odor. The puppy will cuddle right up with the clothing and thus feel somewhat less lonely.

The First Days and Nights

The first night is the worst, for both you and your puppy. It is during the first night that the little Boxer will most miss its littermates. It feels lonely, is often very restless, and whimpers. Don't make the mistake of taking it into your bed. Certainly it will feel happier there because it is close to you, but it will consider your bed its nighttime sleeping place from then on—and that will not be so comfortable for you, particularly once your pet is fully grown. For these reasons, you need to place your dog's designated bed in a spot where it can see you and possibly smell you—at the end

When you lift the puppy, always use one hand to support its hindquarters.

Caution: Never forget to hold the puppy securely. It may seem as still as can be—and then suddenly try to jump out of your arms. For the same reason, also use caution when children want to hold the puppy.

Never Too Young to Learn

A puppy has to learn three lessons right at the outset: it has to become accustomed to the leash (see HOW-TO: Basic Training, page 50), answer to its name, and become housebroken.

Answering to its name: Many breeders give you an opportunity to choose a name for your Boxer. Then the breeder can start early to call the puppy by its name. For you, that has an advantage: In most cases, your puppy already will answer to its name when it comes to your household.

Say your dog's name in a friendly, cheerful voice, never in connection with expressing your disapproval. When the dog obeys, praise it, give it a treat as a reward, or both.

Becoming housebroken: Housebreaking your puppy requires somewhat more effort. Always keep in mind that a housebroken puppy is more a result of your watchfulness and perseverance than of the puppy's tractability.

✔ For these reasons, it is necessary to take the dog outdoors after every nap and meal.

✔ In the morning too, the puppy has to go out as soon as it wakes up. Wait until afterward for a good morning greeting; otherwise, your pet might have an accident.

of your bed, for example. That will also be the easiest way for you to know when the Boxer needs to go out at night, which is definitely a possibility during the early stages.

The adjustment phase: There is no general rule for predicting your puppy's behavior during the first few days and nights. Try to heed the following advice: Observe your dog and learn to understand it. Give it ample time and opportunity to become accustomed to its new home in peace and quiet. Hectic movements and loud yelling can intimidate the puppy in its new environment. Another guideline: During the initial phase, don't show off your new pet to friends and relatives.

Lifting the puppy: If you want to pick up your puppy, there is only one way to go about it (see drawing, above): From behind, place one hand beneath its chest in such a way that all your fingers rest between its forelegs. Support its hindquarters with your other hand.

When you hold the puppy in your arms, make sure that its forelegs are close to its body and do not get bent, for example.

✔ Select a place where your dog can relieve itself, and always take it to the same spot. That will help your pet connect the site with the activity more quickly.

✔ If the puppy was able to wait and succeeded in relieving itself outside, shower it with praise or give it a little treat. That way, "going outside" will always be a pleasant experience for it.

✔ If you keep a close eye on your puppy, you will quickly be able to tell when it has to go. In most cases, it will sniff extensively and turn around in circles. Some puppies also begin to scratch at the door after a short time, or stand at the door whimpering and barking to show that they need to go out.

✔ If a little accident should occur in your home—despite all your vigilance—it will be necessary to quickly and thoroughly clean the spot with a disinfectant, followed by an odor neutralizer. Otherwise, the dog will keep on using that spot. In addition, scold your pet with a vigorous "No" or "Bad dog." In the initial phase, a puppy may make 10 to 20 puddles a day, and you will have to get out of bed several times a night.

Note: The old method of rubbing the puppy's nose in its "business" is both absurd and ineffective.

Nap Time

A young dog also has to learn that it cannot race around and play all the time; it also needs many hours of sleep each day. There are some puppies that are so full of go that they have to be "forced" to sleep. To coax such a puppy to come to its bed, offer it a little snack and use a calm tone of voice. If necessary, sit down beside your pet for a little while. As a general rule, a puppy is so tired after playing that it will fall asleep.

Tip: If your Boxer will not nap of its own accord, do not shut it up alone in a room. It will be miserable, whimper, and be completely unable to calm down. Rather, it has to learn that it can go to sleep with an easy mind and still find its family there when it wakes up. Once your Boxer has developed this trust, it will sleep undisturbed even by the many background noises of your household, including the television, radio, and dishwasher.

Boxers practice typical behavioral patterns as they play together. Here the Boxer on the left is challenging the one on the right to a make-believe fight.

Another spread of various handsome Boxers. Playfulness is a very common personality trait of the breed.

The Boxer's Bed: Its Private Domain

Your dog should associate only positive things with its bed. For that reason you should allow your pet to bring its toys or bones to chew into its bed. Activities such as correcting your pet, giving it medications, and taking its temperature ought to be taboo there. Children also should respect the dog's special place. They need to learn that it belongs exclusively to their four-legged friend and that the Boxer should not be disturbed there.

With Other Dogs

Teaching your pet proper social behavior toward other dogs is of great importance. A puppy can easily become accustomed to associating with other dogs. On the daily walk there will always be ample opportunity to let the puppy play with other dogs. An adult dog in most cases will accept the puppy and play with it.

Make sure the game doesn't get too rough; the puppy might be frightened or even injured. A single negative experience with other dogs can affect its patterns of social behavior. Ask the owners of the other dogs whether their pets are used to associating with puppies. If they are, there is no objection to their playing together. If your puppy has a chance to gain experience in dealing with other dogs, it will have no problems later, as an adult, in associating with other members of its species. Regardless of that, however, you will also find out that dogs, too, have their likes and dislikes.

Being Alone

If you are to avoid having to make extensive changes in your life on account of your new pet—such as giving up going out to dinner or to the movies—then your little four-legged friend has to learn to stay alone on occasion. You cannot leave it alone for hours at a time, however; even a fully grown Boxer should not be left on its own for more than six hours. As soon as your puppy has settled into your home and is familiar with its new surroundings, you can safely try leaving it alone for ten minutes. Gradually you can increase that length of time. It is important for your little four-legged friend to learn that you will always come back.

To indicate complete subjugation, the Boxer that loses the battle over rank order presents its throat to the winner.

CHECKLIST

Things to do Before Buying a Boxer

There are many things that you must consider before taking the plunge and purchasing a Boxer. Following is a list of tips to help you in making your decision.

✔ Talk to experienced Boxer owners first. Not only can they provide you with a wealth of valuable information and tips, but experienced owners can also alert you to potential problems or difficulties that you may not have considered.

✔ Do your research. Information is key when you're considering pet ownership of any kind. In addition to this book, there are many other sources of information on the market specifically geared toward Boxer ownership. Turn to the Information section of this book (page 92). There, you'll find a listing of clubs, books, publications, and websites to aid you in your search. These resources should help answer most of your initial questions and provide access to still more detailed information.

✔ Visit breeders and pet stores. Talk to breeders, dealers, and sales personnel. It's a good idea to jot down a list of questions and concerns before your visit, so as to avoid forgetting to ask something important while you're there. Share ideas, and ask questions about expenses and the amount of time you plan to be able to spend with your new Boxer.

✔ Review your budget. Are you willing to spend the sums necessary to keep a pet Boxer healthy and happy? In addition to your time, love, and care, dogs require

- food
- shelter
- equipment
- supplies
- toys, and especially,
- veterinary care.

These costs can add up, but most dog owners will say they get paid back tenfold.

✔ Finally, and most importantly, determine whether dog ownership, and specifically Boxer ownership, is right for you. Before making a decision that will affect you, your family, and a dog for the rest of your lives, you must consider the situation at length. Make a list of pros and cons. It's a large investment of time and money, so decide if you're ready for the sacrifices and joys that come along with owning a Boxer. Remember, it's like adding someone to your family. If you're ready for ownership of a Boxer, you'll most likely find it a life-changing decision filled with the benefits of loyal companionship and a lifetime of memories.

UNDERSTANDING BOXERS

Not only can Boxers communicate with other dogs, they also can make their emotions and wishes known to humans. Often enough you will intuitively give the correct interpretation to these signals. Alternatively, you can learn over time to interpret them by observing your pet closely.

Body Language

Boxers have a very special way of making themselves understood through body language and mimicry.

Alertness: If an unfamiliar noise, for example, catches your Boxer's interest, it will hold its head at an angle and wrinkle its forehead.

Joy: Boxers, like other dogs as well, express pleasure by wagging their tail.

Contentment: On walks you surely will see time and again how your Boxer, full of delight, throws itself down on the grass and rolls back and forth. It is brimming with exuberance. This behavior is a sign of its well-being. If it feels particularly good, it will lie on its side, totally relaxed. Lying on its back is an expression of absolute intimacy.

Submissiveness: Lying on its back, the Boxer also presents its throat. That is a gesture of submissiveness. You will see it repeatedly

These two can speak volumes with just a look in their eyes.

during fights over rank order as well. The weaker dog lies on its back and presents its throat to the other dog. In this way it demonstrates that it is the underdog. The stronger dog's impulse to bite at it, however, is inhibited by its behavioral makeup. And, after all, the purpose of the dispute—to determine who is top dog—has been fulfilled.

Sadness: If your Boxer is sad, it will curl up in a ball. If you have punished your pet, it may be quite offended. Some Boxers will turn away and fail to react even to treats or kind words.

Fear: A Boxer shows fear by putting its tail between its legs. It reacts with the very same behavior when it has done something naughty and you then call it to come. Its head drooping and its tail tucked between its legs, it slinks toward you.

Expressive eyes: The Boxer's eyes often express its feelings. To interpret these feelings correctly, however, you need to have known your pet for some time: its pleading look when it wants to get hold of a treat; its look of impatience when the daily walk is long overdue; then the happy look in its eyes when your Boxer knows it is being allowed to come along.

Vocalization

The Boxer has available a wide range of barks and other sounds with which it can express its state of mind and its wishes. It is not without good reason that all these utterances are described as vocalization. The more time you spend with your Boxer, the more nuances the dog will express in its communication—and, conversely, the better you will understand your pet.

Whimpering and whining: The Boxer indicates that it is in pain by means of high-pitched tones, produced with its mouth closed. When begging, too, it makes the same sounds—for example, when it wants something to eat or would like to go out.

Growling: When the growling seems more like humming, it is an indication of your Boxer's well-being; but if it is a deep rumble, the Boxer is in a hostile mood and ready for a fight. Deep growling warns the opponent of the impending attack.

Barking: Where barking is concerned, both the timbre and the intervals between barks have information to convey. Even barking in a deep pitch is a sign of greeting, meant in a friendly way. Dislike is expressed by high-pitched, hectic barking.

Governed by Its Instincts

The Boxer's behavior, like that of every other animal, is determined to a great extent by instinctive reactions and drives. In the final analysis, they serve the purpose of self-preservation or preservation of the species.

The instinct to resist enables the dog to defend itself.

The hunting or preying instinct expresses itself when the Boxer chases an animal that is moving away from it and that it therefore views as a quarry. Often this is only a kind of game of tag—for instance, when the Boxer chases a hare. This pattern of behavior is enacted even though the Boxer is not exactly a hunting dog. The Boxer's training has to be aimed at repressing this drive as much as possible. Any impulses in this direction should be put to an end while still in their initial stages—for example, when your Boxer digs in mouse nests or molehills. Similarly, do not let your pet chase deer and other game. To rule out the possibility of your dog being injured, you should consider whether you want to let your pet off its leash in an unenclosed hunting ground.

Tip: However obedient your Boxer may be, you still have to expect that someday it will run after a wild animal in flight. When that happens, do not budge from the spot where your pet ran away from you. Do not run after it. Your Boxer will get its bearings by means of its good sense of smell and will find its way back to you.

Because Boxers occasionally appear to be somewhat dreamy and absentminded, they are also known as the philosophers of the canine world.

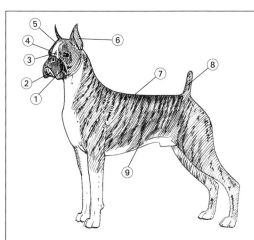

Illustrated Standard

1. Broad, blunt muzzle
2. Undershot bite
3. Shallow wrinkles on forehead when alert
4. Distinct stop
5. Slightly arched skull
6. Ears cropped long and tapering*
7. Slightly sloping topline
8. Tail set high, docked and carried upward
9. Stomach slightly tucked up

❏ **Color:** fawn and brindle, both with or without white flashing and black mask
❏ **DQ:** any color other than fawn or brindle; white markings exceeding one third of entire coat

*Ears may be uncropped, although this may be faulted in the show ring.

The instinct to protect applies not only to the Boxer's offspring, but to its human family as well. On walks it will always check to make sure that its human pack is all accounted for. It grants its protection to children in particular. If you encounter other people with dogs, your

Temperament: Part Heredity, Part Environment

One popular theory of temperament is that when a puppy is born, it will have inherited one of three possible temperaments:
✔ a steady, sound temperament;
✔ an "extreme" temperament (aggressive or overly fearful); or
✔ a temperament that can develop into either one of the previous two, depending on the environment in which the puppy is raised.

It should be said that the school of thought that says puppies are born inherently "good" or "bad" (meaning they will grow up to have the same tempera-ment they were born with, regardless of environment) is shrinking every day. Therefore, most dog experts agree that most pups can go either way, depending on environment.

Fortunately, despite its fierce look, the Boxer is widely considered to have an affable, gentle, and playful temperament that rarely displays aggression toward people unless poorly mistreated. But, that being said, you should keep in mind that in raising a puppy, the environment you create can have a profound influence on the dog's future behavior and temperament.

One adventurous Boxer attempts a swan dive, and a few more "smile" for the camera.

Can You Afford a Boxer?

Dogs are expensive, and Boxers are no exception. The following is a list of expenses you can expect to incur in your first year of owning a Boxer.

Crate (large)	$100
Pad for crate	$50
Baby gates (2)	$80
Pet stain and odor remover (1 gallon [3.8 L])	$20
Various chew toys	$30
"Anti-chewing" spray (16-ounce spray)	$ 7
"Big dog" scoop	$17
Dog food (quality)	$400
Dog bowls (ceramic or no-tip stainless steel) (2)	$20
Dental kit (toothbrush, toothpaste, finger brush)	$6
Adjustable collars (2)	$10
Matching 6-foot (1.8 m) leash	$9
Personalized dog tag	$5
Toenail clippers, styptic powder	$17
Brush	$12
Dog shampoo, conditioner (concentrated; 1 gallon [3.8 L])	$35
Doses of flea and tick control (12)	$72
Heartworm preventive	$120
Routine veterinary care	$200
Obedience classes (10 months)	$200

First Year Total **$1,410**

Other:

Fencing for yard	$300–$1,000+
Dog door	$100–$250
Boarding, kennel (2-week vacation)	$170
Spay/Neuter	$120–$200+

Boxer will become extremely alert. It will plant itself in front of you and bristle its hair. Once the "danger"—that is, the other dog—is past, its level of tension will decrease once more.

The instinct to look after and take care of others concerns primarily the puppies, but it can also extend to the littlest members of your family. It is expressed when the dog licks you—especially your face. For reasons of hygiene, you should not allow it to do so, because the Boxer easily could transmit diseases or worms to you in this way. For this reason, try especially hard to keep the dog from licking your children; offer the Boxer your ear or hands as an alternative.

The instinct to eat serves only one purpose: self-preservation. Nothing is altered by the fact that the Boxer, as a house pet, no longer has to find food for itself, but is fed by its owner.

The mating instinct also has only one purpose: preservation of the species. It cannot be influenced by training.

Boxer Characteristics At a Glance
(compared to other dog breeds)

Characteristic	Rating
Energy level:	▢▢▢
Exercise requirements:	▢▢
Playfulness:	▢▢▢
Affection level:	▢▢▢▢
Friendliness toward dogs:	▢▢
Friendliness toward other pets:	▢▢▢
Friendliness toward strangers:	▢▢
Ease of training:	▢▢
Watchdog ability:	▢▢
Protection ability:	▢▢
Grooming requirements:	▢
Cold tolerance:	▢▢
Heat tolerance:	▢

Out of possible Five (▢▢▢▢▢)

TRAINING: THE GENTLE APPROACH

Developmental Phases

To train your Boxer correctly, you first need to learn something about the process of its development. It occurs in several different phases, each of which is linked to a certain age:

✔ vegetative phase: the first and second weeks of life
✔ transitional phase: the third week
✔ imprinting phase: the fourth through seventh weeks
✔ socialization phase: the eighth through twelfth weeks

In the imprinting phase the puppy's experiences become firmly fixed in its memory. What the puppy learns during this time it will retain all its life. However, what it does not learn it can never make up later on.

In the socialization phase, the dog integrates itself into its environment. Therefore the actual training process can take place during this period of time. That is why breeders let the puppies go to their new homes once they are eight weeks old.

Basic Obedience

In any event, your Boxer needs a basic level of obedience: It has to know the position assigned to it and behave accordingly.

Teaching basic obedience is the first step in welcoming a Boxer to your family.

The family as pack: Because the dog is a pack animal, it interprets its human family also, along with any other pets, as its pack. Within this human/dog pack your Boxer also will instinctively keep trying to climb one rung higher in the hierarchy until it reaches the position of leader. That is reflected, for example, in its attempts to lie on the couch, armchair, or your bed. This is its way of striving to put itself on an equal footing with you. You cannot allow that to happen.

The human as pack leader: One member of the family has to lead the pack. In a dog pack there is always a single leader, and in your human/dog pack you have to take that position. Your Boxer will accept that fact, too, if you get it used to playing a subordinate role from the outset. In the various situations that arise, you will see that the Boxer is actually glad when it repeatedly receives confirmation of the position assigned it within the family. All you have to do is to lead it consistently and firmly toward acceptance of that position.

Consistency Is the Foundation

Your puppy's training begins at the very moment it comes in the door. That is when its acclimation to the human/dog pack starts. The goal of this process is for your Boxer to take its place in the family rather than to dominate the family.

Laying down the rules: You and your family need to agree in advance on what the puppy is allowed to do and what is absolutely against the rules. Include your children in these discussions, too, because consistency in enforcing the rules is the only way for your puppy to fit in successfully. For example, all the family members must present a united front in refusing to give the dog table scraps. Give it a treat from your plate once or twice—and the Boxer will be perpetually begging whenever your family is at the table.

Abiding by the rules: Even if your puppy gives you a look of devotion, don't give in. Just the contrary: whenever your Boxer begs at the table, a sharply uttered reprimand such as "No" is appropriate. Even though that may seem harsh to you, you have to admit that a dog sitting beside the table and drooling is not exactly a pretty sight.

Receptiveness to Learning

The Boxer is not exclusively governed by its instincts and drives. Otherwise, it would be unable to react appropriately to its environment. Its ability to learn puts it in a position to adjust to new situations. It learns by making associations between frequently recurring events and its own experiences during those events, and by firmly anchoring them in its memory. That is why you have to systematically practice a behavior that you want your pet to adopt. Over time, you can teach your Boxer to obey certain commands.

However, the Boxer also learns by observing, as described above. Its excellent powers of observation help it to correctly evaluate recurring situations. If, for example, its owner habitually puts on a coat and shoes before taking the Boxer outdoors, it will eventually learn that a walk is in the offing. If the owner also takes the leash off the hook, the dog knows at once that the moment is at hand—and that it can come along.

Praise and Scolding

Rewards: With all training exercises, there is always a need for praise or, even better, a little treat in addition as a reward. In this way your Boxer will connect the action you want it to perform with a pleasurable consequence for itself—and in time your pet will automatically perform as asked.

If you lavish your little four-legged friend with praise for everything it does correctly, you will achieve the greatest success in the quickest possible way.

Punishment: Whenever your Boxer has failed to comply with one of the

Boxers have great stamina when they run; if they give up quickly and are listless, they may be ill.

To scold a puppy for misbehavior, hold it firmly by the nape and shake.

established rules, however, you have to punish it. In doing so, keep two things in mind:

✔ Avoid physically punishing your Boxer. Verbal reprimand is all your puppy really needs if it acts up. However, as just mentioned, your best bet is to catch your pet in a desirable act and impart lavish praise for a deed well-done. Dogs respond much more readily to praise than they do to negative reinforcement, especially the physical type.

✔ Your puppy will understand an admonition only if it immediately follows the transgression. Therefore, verbally punish your puppy only when you catch it red-handed. Then it can draw some connection between its "misdeed" and the unpleasant aftermath.

Human speech. The best way to express criticism or praise is to talk quite normally with your Boxer! Even though it cannot understand the majority of what you say, your intonation and the way you speak give the dog the message you would like to deliver. Words lovingly spoken tell the Boxer that it has done something right. Harshly uttered words, such as "No," give the dog the signal that you are dissatisfied with it. Don't be disappointed, however, if the dog doesn't immediately react the way you wish. Only with a great deal of patience can you help your Boxer become ready and willing to learn the correct behavior.

Boxers Need to Be Busy

Every dog needs meaningful activity to keep from feeling unneeded and becoming dull and sluggish. If it is not kept occupied, your pet might possibly take out its surplus energy and boredom on your furniture. By virtue of its stamina and temperament, the Boxer is suited for a great many activities.

Keeping Your Boxer Fit and in a Good Mood

Playing with children is always a pleasure for a Boxer; children are its favorite playmates. A puppy—and, later on, the fully grown dog—automatically feels drawn to them. With children it can have a marvelous time romping, having races, and playing ball. A Boxer that is accustomed early on to associating with children and has no negative experiences with them will enjoy playing with them all its life.

Tip: You will see how gently the dog treats the little children and how well it recognizes the difference between adults and children. Nevertheless, do not allow small children to go for a walk alone with a fully grown Boxer.

Playing with other dogs provides two types of training for your Boxer. First, your dog has a chance to let off steam; second, such encounters with four-legged friends foster social contact.

Above: Exercise, including soccer, is vital to your Boxer's good health.

Left: Through its master's gestures and tone of voice, the Boxer grasps what it is being asked to do.

"Tug-of-war" is a common and healthy form of play between Boxers.

This pair of pups looks ready for some attention.

Ouch!

✔ **How common are dog bites?** An estimated 31.2 million families own dogs in the United States, and each year, more than 4.7 million Americans are bitten by dogs. Of these cases, it is estimated that 800,000 (or just over 15%) of these require emergency room treatment.

✔ **Who gets bitten?** Children, mostly. The vast majority of dog bite cases involve children under age 12.

✔ **Who's doing the biting?** It's not who you might suspect. Studies indicate that the majority of dogs biting people are not strays or feral dogs, but dogs that are owned by someone. Furthermore, many of the reported cases come from bites of someone in a family by the family pet.

You can ride a bike with a Boxer as your companion as soon as your pet is fully grown. Its stamina and willingness to run make the Boxer an ideal partner on bicycle excursions.

Of course, you have to slowly introduce the dog to this type of activity. Start with just under 2 miles (3 km) and gradually increase the distance covered to 6 miles (10 km).

Before taking your Boxer on a biking excursion, be sure it is properly obedience trained. Even with such training, always wear a helmet and maintain a slow to moderate pace. Also, if possible, all biking done with your Boxer should be done in parks and off-road trails and off-road paths, not on paved streets. Boxers are such powerful dogs, and if yours decides to dash off in the opposite direction, it could cause you to lose your balance. And the last place you would want this to happen in would be a busy street!

Does jogging appeal to you? Then go jogging with your Boxer! Its physical endurance may turn out to offer you an incentive. In any event, your pet will thoroughly enjoy running along beside you. Incidentally, the type of sport you engage in is basically irrelevant, because only one thing matters to your dog—being with you.

Swimming is fun for some Boxers. They are by no means tireless swimmers, but in hot summer weather they enjoy a cool dip from time to time. They especially like swimming with their master or mistress.

Guarding: If you have a front or back yard, you will get to see your Boxer in the role of guard dog. True, it will simply lie there and observe things, but while doing so its mind is completely on its work, and the Boxer is in its proper element. Incidentally, the Boxer is not a yapper and will not bark at everyone out on the street who passes by its territory. But anyone who walks by property guarded by a Boxer had better think twice before entering the premises unannounced.

Exercises such as drilling the *sit* command or throwing a stick to be fetched should always be made a part of the daily walk.

Agility and Specialized Training in a Dog Club

If you make a concerted effort to drill exercises with your dog and are interested in learning about additional types of activities, you can contact a dog club. For the address of a Boxer training site near you, contact the American Boxer Club (see Information, page 92).

Agility training with a partner: Many dog clubs now offer agility. In this type of dog sport, owner and dog together perform certain exercises, sometimes also in competition with other Boxers and their owners. To create the necessary partner relationship, there must be absolute trust between dog and owner.

The Daily Routine and New Experiences

Keeping to the "schedule": With all the activities that you undertake in order to keep your Boxer occupied, it is important that they take place on a regular basis. Your pet will get used to a regular daily routine. Soon it will know when it is time to be fed and when it is time for its walk. It will then wait for these events to occur.

Trying out unfamiliar situations: It is equally important to introduce your Boxer to a wide variety of situations. It will learn from them and in this way develop the desired strength of character. A dog that is afraid of everything can quickly become a dog that bites when scared.

If you live in the country, just take your Boxer along into town sometime. It will adjust quite well to this new situation and learn to deal with the noise, the cars, and the crowds of people.

How Old Is My Boxer? Dog/Human Age Equivalents

Dog's Age	Human's Age
2 months	14 months
3 months	3 years
6 months	5 years
8 months	9 years
12 months	14 years
18 months	20 years
2 years	24 years
3 years	30 years
4 years	36 years
5 years	40 years
6 years	42 years
7 years	49 years
8 years	56 years
9 years	63 years
10 years	65 years
11 years	71 years
12 years	75 years
13 years	80 years
14 years	84 years
15 years	87 years
16 years	89 years
20 years	95 years

This Boxer is in its element: Curiously, it explores the unknown . . .

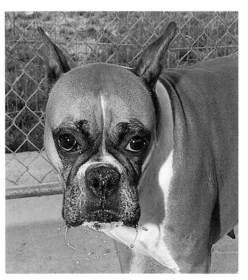

These two show the difference between cropped and uncropped ears (see page 18).

. . . and then takes a cool dip!

Ear cropping is only necessary if you're planning on competing your dog in AKC sanctioned events.

Leash Training
Drawing 1

Your Boxer also has to learn to walk on a leash, or a lead. It should move along at your side, keeping pace with you, without pulling on the leash. As a rule, it is not difficult to accustom a puppy to its collar and leash. To familiarize your puppy with its collar, put it on the Boxer several times a day, for a brief period each time. Praise the dog while it is wearing the collar. In addition, play with your pet to divert it and help it overcome its uneasiness more quickly. After a short time, the collar will cease to bother it.

Next, attach the leash to the collar and take your Boxer for a walk. Hold the leash in your left hand, and have the Boxer walk at your left as well. Only when next to a bicycle should the dog walk on the right, for reasons of safety. Make walking on the leash as pleasant as possible for your Boxer: Praise it or give it a little treat; every young dog is susceptible to that kind of "bribery."

Tip: Never drag the puppy along behind you on its leash if it resists. Especially if that is a frequent occurrence, the dog will associate this negative experience with the leash and consequently try again and again to get the leash off.

Biting on the leash: On your daily walk, make sure that your Boxer is not biting on its leash. That can lead to the loss of a tooth and, in addition, this practice is a disadvantage in the show ring (see Showing Your Boxer, page 87). Moreover, the leash is not a toy on which your Boxer can pull and tug according to its fancy. Certainly it looks comical when the puppy strains against the leash with all its might, but keep in mind that one day it will be bigger and therefore stronger. Then it will cease to be a game: your pet will be taking you for a walk, instead of the other way around.

The Sit Command
Drawing 2

The Boxer should respond to the *sit* command by sitting down on its hindquarters. Your dog has to perform this obedience exercise whenever you want to put on its leash, give it a treat, or prepare to cross a street with it. Start the lesson in the context of giving the Boxer a treat. Do not let your pet have the treat until it is sitting down. You will see that the Boxer carries out the command very quickly when there is the prospect of a reward. If your pet does not sit down right away, help things along by gently pressing down on its rump.

1) On a leash, the dog walks at its companion's left, at the same pace, without tugging at the leash.

2) To reinforce the sit command, gently press the dog's rear toward the ground.

The Down Command
Drawing 3

Whereas sitting on command should be performed only for short spans of time, the *down* position is intended for longer periods. Your Boxer should assume this position when you leave it alone briefly or when you are seated at the dinner table.

Upon hearing the command *Down*, the dog should lie down so that its hind legs are bent and its forelegs are stretched straight out. A puppy is still too young to be taught this obedience exercise. As a young dog—by the age of six months at the latest—the Boxer can master it, however.

When teaching this lesson, you have to expect that your Boxer will balk at first. Then you can simply help matters along a bit: as you command *Down*, tug the leash toward the ground without exerting force. And of course the same rule applies here as with all the other exercises: Every successfully executed command is to be followed by a reward.

Breaking Bad Habits

Jumping up: Jumping up on people, which is typical of Boxers, is an annoying problem. Bubbling over with joy and high spirits, Boxers love to jump up in order to get closer to their loved ones. You have to make it clear to your pet that it can be just as full of enthusiasm on all fours. If it jumps up on you, push it down and pat it when it has all four feet on the

3) *When it hears the down command, the Boxer should assume this position.*

ground. Lend added emphasis with the words "Good dog, stay down" or "Don't jump up." Further, ask all family members and friends to follow exactly the same procedures. Once your Boxer has formed the habit of jumping up, you will have trouble getting it to unlearn such behavior. Nevertheless, it is advisable that you do so. Your Boxer might one day jump up on a passerby, and that could lead to difficulties and prove costly as well.

Damaging the furnishings: Your Boxer has to learn that it is not allowed to scratch at doors, chew on furniture, and bite rugs and other objects to pieces. If you catch your pet working away at a table leg with relish, give it a shake (see drawing, page 43) and back that up with a sharp "No" or "Bad dog." To keep the Boxer from temptation, give it toys to occupy it.

DAILY GROOMING AND HEALTH CHECK

Your Boxer needs a daily grooming routine. Get it accustomed to this process while still a puppy. Quite likely, however, your pet will already have become familiar with such procedures at the breeder's, where it was weighed and kept clean daily. In any event, it is very important that your dog submit to all the grooming procedures you institute. That includes allowing you to put your hand in its mouth, because you have to be able at all times to take something out of the Boxer's mouth. You also have to be able to give the dog tablets or drops.

The Boxer's daily grooming includes the care of its coat, eyes, ears, and nails. This daily ritual is intended primarily to keep the Boxer healthy and content, but it simultaneously promotes contact with the dog's "significant human."

Routine Examination

Additionally, a periodic check to detect signs of possible disease can be linked with daily hygienic measures: Owners who spend a great deal of time with their pet will be able to tell whether the dog really feels well. Especially while performing the various steps of the daily grooming routine, you have an excellent opportunity to check specifically for indica-

Grooming your Boxer on a regular basis will give you opportunity for brief health exams.

tions of health problems. It is best to go through the following checklist each time:
✔ Are the Boxer's eyes clear and clean, or is a sticky discharge present? Do its eyes tear? Are they reddened?
✔ Are its ears free of parasites?
✔ Is its coat glossy and close fitting? Is it dull? Is it bare in patches?
✔ Is the dog listless or sluggish?

Fleas and Other Parasites

Parasites are organisms that receive nutriment from the bodies of other living creatures. Among the animals they infest are Boxers. If you find parasites on your Boxer, you need to treat it immediately.

Worms

Worms can cause vomiting, diarrhea, and weight loss. In puppies, they also lead to disturbances of growth. An unmistakable sign of worm infestation in a puppy is an overly distended abdomen. Your veterinarian can definitely diagnose worm infestations through the microscopic examination of your pet's stool. The type of parasite involved will determine treatment.

Heartworms: Heartworm disease is a devastating parasitic disease of dogs that is found throughout the country. Transmitted from dog to dog by mosquitoes, the heartworm larvae gain entrance into the body and begin a migration to the heart and vessels of the host dog. Once they reach the heart, heartworm larvae mature within the organ itself and within the blood vessels of the lungs. They then reproduce, shedding new larvae into the bloodstream to be picked up by a feeding mosquito and subsequently transferred to another unfortunate dog, thereby completing the life cycle.

Left untreated, heartworm infestation can lead to breathing difficulties, weakness, and heart failure in affected dogs. Although newer, safer treatments for this disease are now available, your best bet is prevention. Special preventive medications can be administered orally or topically once a month. These are readily available from your veterinarian. As an added bonus, most of these medications also contain ingredients that prevent intestinal parasitism at the same time.

Fleas

Fleas feed on a dog by biting it and sucking its blood. Their bites often cause severe itching and, above all, skin infections. Open sores resulting from the dog's biting and scratching are an ideal breeding ground for

Zoonotic Diseases

Don't worry, it's still safe to go to the zoo—you don't have to be there to pick up a zoonotic disease. But these are diseases that can be passed on from your Boxer to you. These can include rabies, Lyme disease, and worm infestation. Don't panic, this is fairly uncommon, but it's something you should be aware of with a dog in your home.

pathogens. Because fleas migrate from one dog to another, transmission of disease is within the realm of possibility. Fleas love warm weather, but they can appear in either summer or winter.

If your Boxer scratches itself incessantly, it may have fleas. You can conduct a flea inspection by carefully scrutinizing the dog's coat. Check it on a regular basis. Fleas are visible to the naked eye.

Treatment: Topical once-a-month flea products for dogs are now available through veterinarians and are highly effective at controlling fleas when used in combination with environmental flea control.

Tip: Always treat the dog's bed and the surrounding area with an insecticidal spray when you treat for fleas. Fleas, along with their eggs, often settle in blankets and bedding.

Mites

Mites (mange) can be found anywhere on the body of affected dogs but tend to be worse on the neck, ears, and face. The external signs of a mite infestation can include scratching, hair loss, and scab formation. However, contrary to popular belief, not all types of mange cause itching. Demodectic mange will not cause a dog to scratch unless a second bacterial infection is present. For this reason, be sure to have your veterinarian examine all cases of hair loss affecting your dog to be sure mange mites are not involved.

Treatment: If you think your pet has mites, take it to the veterinarian. He or she will be able to tell what kind of mite is involved and initiate treatment. The presence of ear mites can cause a dark, dirty, waxy material to adhere to the inner skin of the ear. Ear mites can cause your pet a great deal of discomfort, as evidenced by excessive ear scratching or violent head shaking. See your veterinarian immediately.

Tip: Before traveling abroad, find out what parasites might endanger your dog at your destination, and ask your veterinarian for the appropriate medications that can be used to protect your Boxer during the trip.

Ticks

These parasites usually appear in the spring. They lodge themselves firmly in the Boxer's skin and suck themselves full of blood. As they do so, their original size increases fivefold. You need to examine your pet for ticks after every walk. Ticks like to get into a Boxer's large ears. But don't confuse these with the much smaller ear mites.

Treatment: If you find a tick, first kill it using a flea and tick spray, then remove it immediately by grasping the entire head and body and pulling it directly out of your pet's skin. Pet stores sell special tick tweezers that make such removal easy. When removing the tick, the most important thing is to make sure that the head comes out along with the body; otherwise, infection can result. Should that occur, take the dog to the veterinarian right away.

Lyme disease and ehrlichicsis are serious, potentially fatal diseases that affect warm-blooded animals and humans. Because your Boxer should walk and play in parks or other wooded areas, the possibility of exposure to Lyme disease must be considered. The ailment can even be contracted in your pet's own backyard.

Lyme disease, first identified in Lyme, Connecticut, is spread primarily by the deer tick,

Mosquitoes and Heartworm

During mosquito season, all dogs should be on heartworm prevention once a month. Monthly preventives don't stay in the dog's system for an entire month, but rather attack all heartworms in one particular stage of development. So, giving your dog a heartworm prevention pill once a month whenever mosquitoes are around will ensure that no heartworms will ever mature.

The most common way of testing for heartworm is to check the blood for circulating microfilariae (the immature form of heartworms), but this method can be innacurate in as many as 20% of all tested dogs. A more accurate way is a method that detects antigens to heartworms in the blood.

With either test, the presence of heartworms is not detectable until at lesast six months after infection. Heartworms are treatable in their early stages, but there are more treatments being developed. If left untreated, heartworms can be fatal to your pet.

a tiny bloodsucker credited with carrying an illness that can do your Boxer, and you, great physical harm! Borelliosis (the medical name of this disease) can affect your dog in several ways, but usually swelling and tenderness around the joints is observable.

If you have been bitten by a tick or see the telltale tick bite with its characteristic surrounding of red (somewhat like a bull's-eye on a target), consult your physician or county health department. Timely diagnosis and treatment are essential.

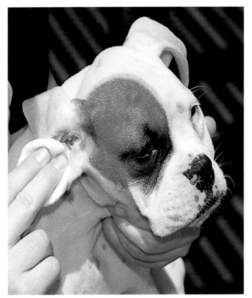

Use a fresh cloth with a cleansing solution when cleaning your Boxer's ears.

Boxers typically have a strong desire to please you.

The only thing this perfect Boxer seems to be missing is an identification tag.

One of the best ways for a Boxer to stay healthy is to get enough exercise.

HOW–TO: GROOMING

Grooming of your Boxer won't take much time, but it should be performed regularly.

Eye Check

The Boxer's eyes have to be clear. The eyes of this breed in particular are somewhat sensitive. A draft—created when the dog rides in a car with the windows open, for example—may well result in conjunctivitis.

Conjunctivitis: The affected eye will begin to tear. The inflammation can be cured with an ophthalmic ointment.

Ectropion: Some Boxers are afflicted with this condition, in which the lower eyelid droops slightly. That causes increased secretion of lacrimal fluid. Drafts may also be a contributing factor. A flow of tears ensues. If it becomes chronic, skin irritations and hair loss may occur in the muzzle area.

If you detect these symptoms, have your pet's eyes examined by the veterinarian, who will prescribe special ointments. Before application, clean the dog's eyes very carefully with a damp cloth, making sure not to rub.

Cleaning the Ears
Drawing 1

The ears have to be checked regularly, and any wax and dirt particles need to be removed. Some Boxers tend to secrete large amounts of wax, whereas others produce none at all.

To clean the ears, it is best to use a commercial ear cleaning solution. Do not use cotton swabs to get deeper into the ear. They could easily injure the inner portion of the ear, which is extremely sensitive.

In any event, the Boxer seldom gets dirt in its ear, which is quite short and floppy. Particularly with ears of this type, however, more frequent ear checks are necessary. Because air flow is relatively poor, inflammations arise more readily, and they have to be treated by a veterinarian.

Your Boxer may also suffer from ear mites (see Fleas and Other Parasites, page 53). If so, it will constantly scratch and scrape at its ears. Take your pet to the veterinarian: only he or she can provide you with the proper medications to bring relief and healing.

Cleaning the Mouth
Drawing 2

The lips need to be cleaned after every meal, to prevent food remnants from accumulating in the folds of the muzzle and possibly causing inflammation. Use a moistened hand towel to wipe between the Boxer's lips and its teeth.

Cleaning the Feet

This is particularly important after a walk in winter; otherwise, thawing salt, sand, and gravel will irritate the skin.

1) Clean the ears with a cloth dipped in oil.

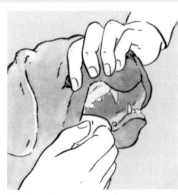

2) After the dog eats, clean its mouth with a soft cloth.

In addition, regular foot care should include checking between your pet's toes. If you fail to remove small pebbles and other dirt particles, small injuries to the balls of the toes can result, and they can become inflamed.

The nails should be clipped by the veterinarian, who has the ability to determine precisely where the quick lies and where the dead keratin begins. If your pet frequently runs on concrete, its nails usually get worn down on their own.

The pads of the feet need no special care, but in winter, rub them with vaseline to keep them supple. Make sure not to use too much of these moisturizers. Otherwise, the pads of the feet will become too soft, and may tear.

Coat Care
Drawing 3

Every few days, groom the Boxer's coat with a so-called hound-glove, a rubber currycomb, a good brush, or a chamois cloth.

✔ With the rubber currycomb, brush the dog's coat against its natural lie. Give it a good going-over. Most of the hairs that come off will stay in the currycomb.

✔ Use the brush to go over the coat once more, this time *with* the lie of the hair.

✔ Finally, rub your Boxer all over with the chamois or hound-glove.

Be sure to brush the dog's abdomen, neck, and inner thighs as well. The intense mechanical working over of the entire coat stimulates the circulation of the skin. As a result, the coat acquires a velvety gloss.

Replacement of the hair coat: Twice a year the Boxer grows a new coat of hair. Unlike the German Shepherd and Rottweiler, for example, it lacks an undercoat to protect it from variations in temperature.

3) Using the rubber currycomb, vigorously brush the Boxer's coat against the lie of the hair.

When you brush the Boxer's coat as directed at the start of the cold and warm seasons, you will be amazed to see how many hairs are shed. At these times of year, brush your dog daily to spare yourself the job of constantly removing the hairs from furniture and clothing.

Bathing

When? Generally, you should bathe your Boxer only when it is absolutely necessary— for example, when the dog is extremely dirty and has an unpleasant smell. You need to exhibit restraint because every bath affects the natural protective coating of the skin. Generally, because the Boxer's coat is so short, a rubdown with a chamois or a towel after every walk is sufficient.

How? When you bathe your Boxer, use a mild shampoo for dogs. At the end of the bath, your pet has to be rinsed off thoroughly. Be careful not to let shampoo get in the dog's eyes, ears, or mouth. Then, dry the dog well and keep it indoors for the next few hours, to keep it from catching cold.

Tip: Do not bathe a puppy until after its first birthday. Remove any dirt with baby oil and a thorough brushing.

PROPER NUTRITION AND FEEDING

This chapter deals with the feeding and nutrition of fully grown dogs. You have already been given nutritional information for puppies (see Advantages of Buying from a Breeder, page 18). The feeding of a pregnant or lactating bitch is a special topic, which you can read about elsewhere (see Information, page 92).

Commercial Dog Food

Premium, highly digestible commercial dog food is the easiest way to give your dog a balanced, appropriate diet. If you stick to the recommended daily amounts listed on the packaging, you can be certain that your Boxer is getting all the necessary vitamins, minerals, trace elements, proteins, and other important supplements in the right quantities and proper ingredients.

Commercial dog food has yet another advantage. Most products of this kind can be served in either moist or dry form, and that makes them suitable for taking along on trips.

Tip: Especially during the summer months, it is a good idea to feed your pet dry food. That way you will keep odors from forming and attracting flies and other insects.

Kitchen counters are fair game when your Boxer is hungry, so be sure to keep food out of reach.

When Buying Dog Food

A great number of dog food products from various manufacturers are available commercially. Ideally, commercial dog food should contain:
✔ no flavor or fragrance enhancers; they lead the dog to develop an excessive appetite, which ultimately results in extra poundage that is detrimental to its health;
✔ no artificial preservatives, as these may cause allergic reactions;
✔ no coloring agents; they are meant more to appeal to the eye of the buyer—the Boxer attaches no importance to brightly colored vegetable flakes.

Buy quality: Don't try to be thrifty. A well-prepared, nutritionally balanced commercial dog food comes at a price. If you buy a dog food of lower quality, your Boxer might refuse to eat it. If your Boxer is thriving, gaining weight, and not suffering from diarrhea, then you have found the right dog food.

Freshly Prepared Dog Food

It may be that your Boxer does not enjoy commercial dog food as a steady diet. If your pet is a gourmet and wants something special in its bowl from time to time, feed it fresh food that you yourself prepare. That is not altogether easy, because:

✔ You need a source of supply. Not every butcher is willing to give you scraps from his shop.

✔ You have to add the required vitamins, trace elements, and minerals to the food in the right quantities and composition.

✔ The food has to be cooked or at least boiled in water or broth in order to kill any organisms present—and the smell may not be to everyone's liking.

Guidelines for Home-prepared Meals

If you feed your dog a home-prepared meal, be sure to supplement its diet daily with a balanced vitamin/mineral supplement. Also, choose only the finest ingredients when preparing your dog's rations.

Meat absolutely has to be bought with an eye to quality control. You can purchase fresh meat from a butcher or frozen meat in the larger pet stores. Frozen meat has the advantage of being packaged in serving-size amounts and already cut up. All you have to do is thaw a suitable portion, cook it or heat it in water or broth, and add the other ingredients. You can feed your pet beef, lamb, poultry, or venison.

Caution: Pork, if used at all, always should be cooked until completely done, but it is better not to feed your dog pork. It could contain the deadly trichina nematode, which causes trichinosis.

Fish also may be included in your dog's diet. It supplies protein of high nutritive value.

Dairy products: Farmer cheese and cottage cheese are also excellent additions to your Boxer's feeding program. Cow's milk is a valuable food for dogs. It is best to add a teaspoon of honey to the milk and serve it lukewarm.

Tip: Use only low-fat milk, however; otherwise, it will cause diarrhea in your Boxer.

Eggs: One egg yolk or one hard-boiled egg per week should also be included in your dog's meal plan.

Cereal products: Rice, barley, and noodles are well liked by Boxers, and they round out the meal. Unhusked rice (paddy rice) can also be served when your dog is on a special diet, because it acts as a powerful dehydrant.

The most important item in the Boxer's diet is water. It always has to be fresh and, ideally, should be filtered.

Vegetables are part of any balanced feeding program. Easy-to-use kinds include carrots, tomatoes, zucchini, fennel, cauliflower, and all leafy vegetables. Watercress may also be used, though only in small amounts. Legumes like peas, beans, and lentils are not suitable. Vegetables should be steamed briefly. Overcooking reduces the vitamin content, while undercooking can cause stomach upset.

Fruits: All kinds of fruits can be fed to your pet. With certain fruits, remember to remove the pit. In winter, a few orange wedges each day will provide the requisite amount of vitamin C.

Fat and oil are also essential components of your Boxer's nutritional plan. Vegetable oils, which are higher in unsaturated fatty acids, are easier to digest. As little as 1 tablespoon of oil added to the dog's food each day will improve its coat. Sunflower oil or thistle oil are best for this purpose.

Vitamins: The following foods contain the essential vitamins in relatively high concentrations:

✔ Vitamin A: carrots, parsley, tomatoes, spinach, leafy vegetables, milk, fish, egg yolk, and butter

✔ Vitamin B: yeast, milk, liver, heart, leafy vegetables, eggs

✔ Vitamin C: citrus fruits, parsley, spinach, milk
✔ Vitamin D: cod-liver oil (add to your pet's food only in winter)

Seasonings

Iodized table salt is healthful in small quantities unless your Boxer suffers from a heart condition. The seasonings people love, however—pepper, paprika, and the like—are not good for their pets, even in minute quantities.

Bones and Treats

Bones of any kind are not suitable for Boxers. True, with its powerful set of teeth, a Boxer is easily able to utterly demolish bones. Bone splinters can cause life-threatening internal injuries, however. That is why all veterinarians are opposed to feeding bones to dogs.

Nylon or rawhide bones, available in every pet store, make a good substitute. They are suitable for dogs and easy to digest, and they also will keep your pet's teeth clean. Even a puppy can be given an artificial bone to satisfy its urge to chew and to keep it amused.

Bread that has hardened is something that Boxers dearly love to nibble on.

Rawhide bones satisfy the dog's urge to chew and also keep its teeth clean. They are suitable even for puppies.

Now and then, try to treat your dog to fresh, cold running water.

Dog biscuits do more than satisfy your dog's hunger. The large, coarse ones in particular serve to help clean the teeth.

Tip: After the final meal of the day, go ahead and give your Boxer one or two dog biscuits, but be sure to add these calories to the daily total.

Snacks are available in a wide assortment. Here, of course, your individual dog's taste plays a role. Naturally you will not give your dog chocolate of any kind. Pet stores offer a broad range of suitable products, and you can choose between sweet and savory tastes. You should not view these snacks as a substitute for food, however, but as true rewards.

Tip: Keep in mind that treats mean extra calories, and they have to be counted as such if your dog is on a special diet.

Feeding Your Boxer

How often? Generally, an eight-week-old puppy still has to be fed at least twice a day. A fully grown dog, however, can get by on one feeding per day. It is preferable, however, to divide the daily ration into two meals. That way the dog does not ingest too much food at one time, and its stomach is not overloaded. Don't make the mistake of setting out the full bowl for your pet in the morning, so that it can help itself whenever it likes.

When? You can determine the feeding time in accordance with your daily routine. It is a

After a big meal, it's time for a nap!

Right: If the play of its ribs is clearly visible, the Boxer is not overweight.

Below: Meals should be fed at least twice a day, using high-quality food.

—— TIP ——

Important Rules for Feeding

1. Feed your Boxer one or two times daily.

2. Always feed your pet at the same times of day.

3. Do not feed your dog by hand. Your Boxer should have its own bowl.

4. The food should be at room temperature. Never give a dog food straight from the refrigerator.

5. Your Boxer needs to have a good appetite. If it stands listlessly in front of its bowl and pokes around in the food or perhaps picks out certain items, take the bowl away. Although it may sound heartless, let the Boxer go hungry—it will eat the next meal all the more readily.

6. Don't offer the dog any substitutes for its regular diet; you will produce a finicky pet. At each regular meal you will be wondering "Is the Boxer going to eat or not?" Once you have offered your pet a substitute, which it may have found even tastier than its standard meal, you will have to keep resorting to special tidbits to induce the dog to eat.

7. Base the amount you serve on the dog's actual appetite. If your Boxer doesn't finish its meal, the portion was too large; reduce it. If it keeps licking its bowl, however, it is perfectly all right to increase the amount as long as your Boxer doesn't begin to gain weight due to the increased ration.

8. Have your Boxer rest for one hour after every meal.

good idea to feed your pet in the morning and in the evening. In any case, however, you need to stick to whatever feeding schedule you adopt.

Important: After you feed your Boxer, it needs to rest for an hour, so that it can digest its meal.

For a Thirsty Dog

The most important item in your Boxer's diet is water. Sometimes a dog can go without food for several days without any difficulties, but it can never get by without water. The danger that your pet would become dehydrated is enormous.

Always give your Boxer fresh water. Don't just keep filling up its water bowl; clean the bowl thoroughly every day to keep bacteria from accumulating there.

Caution: Make sure that your Boxer does not drink from bodies of standing water, including puddles. The stagnant water can contain disease-causing organisms.

Proper Nutrition for Young Dogs

The feeding of a puppy (animals up to six months in age) usually is up to the breeder or seller initially, and it can vary widely. Ask your seller what the puppy was fed up to the time it joined your family, and feed it exactly the same diet during its first weeks in your home. Pet stores now sell excellent products, specially formulated by the pet food industry, for rearing puppies and young dogs. Many breeders prefer them because they are nutritionally balanced. But whatever you feed your pet, the following rules apply:

✔ Food for puppies has to be high in protein.

✔ In addition, dogs need calcium in this early stage of life. It is important for their permanent set of teeth, which come in roughly by the end of the fourth month, and for bone formation, which occurs during the first year of life.

Proper Nutrition for Old Dogs

When your Boxer is getting on in years (older than six years), you need to make a change in its diet. Today many pet food manufacturers offer products specially formulated for such "senior" dogs.

Feed your older Boxer several times a day. One meal per day can sometimes place too much stress on aging digestive organs.

If Your Boxer Is Too Fat

Why get rid of excess weight? Being overweight is detrimental to your Boxer's health. In your pet as well, excess poundage is a civilizational disease. Too much food, including too many between-meal treats in particular, and too little exercise lead to serious weight gain in a Boxer—and once the Boxer is too fat, it is no longer able to get enough exercise. Inactivity, in turn, has a negative effect on the dog's organs, ligaments, tendons, and muscles.

Is my pet overweight? You can determine without a doubt whether your Boxer is too fat. If its ribs are no longer discernible, it is carrying excess poundage. In a Boxer of normal weight, however, you can clearly see the play of the ribs (see photo, page 65). From behind your pet, lay your hands on either side of its chest. You should be able to easily detect the

path of the ribs when you press lightly on the Boxer's chest. If you have to exert greater pressure to reach the ribs, your Boxer is unmistakably too fat.

The size of your Boxer, however, also has some bearing on your conclusion. A small representative of the breed, naturally, should not produce a reading of much more than 70 pounds (31.8 kg) on the scales, and a female need not necessarily weigh the same as a male (see The AKC Breed Standard, page 7).

How can my dog lose weight? To reduce the excessive poundage effectively, a change in diet is a must! Special diets available from veterinarians can assist in rapid weight loss for your Boxer. Simply feeding a "light" or "less active" formula from your grocery store or pet store will not be enough to stimulate significant weight loss in the overweight pet. Instead, an actual reduction diet should be fed exclusively for six to eight weeks or until the desired weight is lost. Weigh your dog at least once per week to monitor progress. Resist the temptation to offer any treats or snacks, other than perhaps some freshly steamed vegetables (however, these should be offered only in moderation and according to your veterinarian's instructions). After the desired weight loss has been achieved, your pet can then be placed on a less active or light formula to help maintain its "new look."

In addition to dietary modulation, increasing the number of calories burned each day is important in shedding excess poundage and in maintaining the desired weight once it is achieved. As a result, plan on putting your Boxer on a routine and consistent program of daily exercise (see Boxers Need to Be Busy, page 43).

PREVENTIVE HEALTH CARE AND ILLNESSES

There are a number of contagious diseases that your Boxer easily can contract, and they can become life threatening. Vaccination offers effective protection against them.

Vaccinations

Your Boxer puppy should have received its initial immunizations from the seller at or around eight weeks of age. In addition, it needs to receive booster immunizations both at twelve weeks and at sixteen weeks of age (see Vaccination Schedule, page 70). For Boxers over one year of age, follow the vaccination schedule recommended by your veterinarian.

Tip: If you have questions about special situations—for example, if you are planning to have your bitch bred—your veterinarian will be happy to help by providing appropriate advice. Also ask your veterinarian for information about the vaccine used to inoculate your Boxer.

The vaccination certificate of your Boxer records every inoculation given the dog (see What the Buyer Needs to Know, page 15). It also will serve as a reminder of the date the next shot is due. At dog shows and on trips abroad with your Boxer, the vaccination certificate is an indispensable document.

No matter how much attention you pay to your pet, there's no substitute for quality veterinary care.

Worming

No dog is safe from worm infestation, and these parasites can cause enormous health problems (see Fleas and Other Parasites, page 53). Therefore you need to check your dog for worms on a regular basis. Discuss with your veterinarian about administering worm treatments after the first eight weeks of life. At least once a year, bring a stool sample to your veterinarian (who will provide you with appropriate containers for that purpose). If your pet is found to have worms, the veterinarian will prescribe the proper remedy.

As mentioned previously, most heartworm preventatives also contain medications to control intestinal worms. This is just one more good reason to administer such medication to your Boxer.

How to Tell if Your Dog Is Ill

If you know your Boxer well, you will quickly detect any deviations from its normal state of health and behavior. Certain symptoms are considered warning signs of possible disease:

✔ Does its coat show any changes?
✔ Does your pet suffer from lack of appetite?
✔ Does it exhibit continual fatigue?
✔ Does it deliberately creep away and hide?
✔ Is its behavior characterized by sluggishness and dullness?

✔ Is it ill-humored?

✔ Does it display, contrary to its nature, exaggerated fearfulness?

✔ Is it restless for no apparent reason?

✔ Does it whimper and howl strangely, for no obvious reason?

If one of these symptoms is present, there is no need to rush to the veterinarian's office. The cause of the unusual behavior may be entirely harmless. The dog's nose, for example, may be dry after digging in the ground, after sleeping, on very hot days, and even, at times, in a bitch in heat. In all of these cases, however, the nose will be cool and moist again a short time later.

Tip: First, keep a very close eye on your Boxer if you detect any indications of a possible illness. Above all, take your pet's temperature. If the dog has fever or if one or more symptoms begin to worsen, it is time to visit the veterinarian.

When a Veterinarian's Help Is Essential

There are, however, some symptoms that call for an immediate trip to the veterinarian:

Symptoms that usually indicate a medical emergency include breathing difficulties, bleeding, non-weight-bearing lameness, unconscious-

Typical Vaccination Schedule for Preventive Health Care

Serum to prevent:	Basic Series of Initial Immunizations for Your Boxer			
	Week 8	Week 12	Week 16	16 Months
Distemper	x	x	x	x
Parvovirus	x	x	x	x
Parainfluenza	x	x	x	x
Infectious Canine Hepatitis	x	x	x	x
Leptospirosis (Optional)	x	x	x	x
Coronavirus (Optional)	x	x	x	
Rabies			x	x

* For adult Boxers, check with your veterinarian concerning proper vaccination schedules.

Important: Vaccinations do not grant immunity instantaneously. It takes one to two weeks following an initial immunization for immunity to develop.

ness, extreme weakness or lethargy, protracted vomiting (vomiting more than three times within a 60-minute period), bloody diarrhea, abdominal pain, seizures, paralysis, or facial swelling.

Gastric torsion: All large dog breeds, including Boxers, can in isolated cases develop the dreaded gastric torsion (bloat) after eating. Accumulation of gas in the stomach, excessive amounts of food, or overly large pieces of food can cause the stomach to "tilt," twisting about 180 degrees. You can spot this problem by the dog's greatly distended abdomen and pronounced indisposition. In such a case, get your pet to the veterinarian posthaste.

When You Can Treat Your Pet Yourself

You should only attempt to treat your pet yourself after you have first consulted with your veterinarian. While it is true that pet owners can address many minor conditions or procedures at home, your veterinarian should still be made aware of your pet's condition. Remember: A seemingly minor clinical sign or symptom could be a mild outward manifestation of a serious underlying disorder. Also, don't administer a home remedy or over-the-counter medication without first talking with your veterinarian. He or she can provide you with proper information on dosage and method of administration.

Hip Dysplasia

Hip dysplasia (HD) is a typical disorder of medium-size and large dog breeds. Boxers too are susceptible to it. HD is an inherited defect of the hip joint, which—depending on the severity of the case—can lead to weakening

or even paralysis of the hind legs. The symptoms are as follows:

✔ Rising from a sitting or lying position is painful for the Boxer.

✔ Climbing stairs also causes it pain.

✔ Physical exertion causes it to tire quickly.

✔ Over relatively long distances, the Boxer runs fast and hops.

✔ It has trouble jumping.

The condition can be definitely diagnosed only by an X ray, which can be taken once the dog has reached 24 months of age. Any pain and inflammation that may appear can be eased with medication prescribed by the veterinarian. For serious, persistent discomfort, surgical insertion of an artificial hip joint generally has good results. One preventive measure has proved valuable: Do not feed the growing dog too rich a diet.

On Aging and Dying

You will see that your Boxer alters with increasing age. Its exuberant temperament will become calmer, its step will grow slower, its vision and hearing will become weaker, and more and more gray hairs will appear—your dog is getting old. It will sleep a great deal and seek contact with you with mounting frequency. Go along with the changes in its needs, and be considerate of its infirmities. Your Boxer requires your loving care now, and it has a great need for peace, quiet, and security.

The following health problems appear with great frequency in old Boxers—and here's what you can do to alleviate them:

✔ Signs of wear and tear in joints and in the spinal column: always keep the Boxer warmly covered; take shorter, but more frequent, walks.

An eye test.

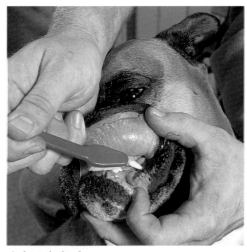

A dental check-up.

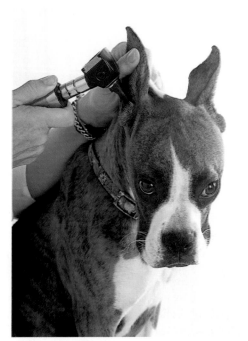

Examining the dog's ear.

Trimming the nails.

✔ Cardiac and circulatory insufficiency: make sure your pet doesn't overdo things, and calm it down when excited.

✔ Bad teeth: give your Boxer nylon bones more often (see Bones and Treats, page 63) or clean its teeth with a toothbrush.

Having the veterinarian put it to sleep. Sooner or later the day will come when you realize that your Boxer is suffering from its infirmities and that there is no hope of remedying its painful condition. When that time arrives, you should consider having your dog put to sleep. The veterinarian will give your Boxer an injection containing an overdose of a tranquilizer, and that will ensure your pet a painless death. Don't leave your Boxer alone at this moment. Pick up your pet and hold it tight; the dog will feel your touch and go peacefully to sleep.

Keep in Touch with Your Veterinarian

There are few diseases and illnesses to which your Boxer is particularly prone. In these cases, only your veterinarian may help. Pay special attention to the following:

✔ **Pyloric stenosis** is a condition where the sphincter, a valve that controls the food flow from the stomach, is much too powerful and prevents any solid food from leaving the stomach. This condition is often seen in pups being weaned and presented with solids for the very first time. It can, however, also develop as a chronic problem in growing Boxers.

Sign: Vomiting of solid food.

Treatment: Surgery.

✔ **Cushing's syndrome:** Due to an overactive adrenal gland, located near the kidneys, the

When the heat is really getting to you, panting is the only thing that helps.

Boxer loses hair evenly on both sides of the body and legs and quickly gains a potbelly. This syndrome is often seen in Boxers eight years or older. Boxers that are on long-term corticosteroid therapy can also develop this syndrome.

Sign: Excessive thirst; weakness of the abdominal muscles.

Treatment: Veterinary care is necessary.

✔ Deafness: Because of a genetic predisposition for deafness associated with excessive white coloration in Boxers, the breed standard disqualifies Boxers with total white markings exceeding one-third of the entire coat. This phenomenon is caused by the absence of pigment cells within the ear that results in nerve deafness as early as six weeks of age. Although not all "white" Boxers are affected, up to 40 percent can suffer from hearing impairment. Blindness is also known to occur in white Boxers, although quite infrequently.

Treatment: None. Needless to say, white Boxers should be neutered to prevent the passage of this undesirable genetic trait to subsequent generations.

✔ Cancer: Boxers seem to have a higher incidence of cancer than do many other breeds. This is believed to be due to an inherent immune, metabolic, or biochemical defect in the Boxer's makeup. Tumors frequently seen in Boxers include mast cell tumors, aortic/carotid body tumors, tracheal tumors, histiocytomas, hemangiomas, melanomas, and lymphosarcomas. General signs associated with cancer in dogs include unexplained weight loss, sudden loss of appetite, chronic lethargy, obvious lumps or masses growing on or beneath the skin, breathing difficulties, persistent discharges, unexplained lameness, or any changes in elimination habits. If any abnormal signs

appear, don't hesitate to consult your veterinarian. If detected and treated in their early stages, many cancers are completely curable.

✔ Spondylosis deformans is a degenerative disease seen in older Boxers characterized by a build-up of calcium deposits along the vertebral column, which put pressure on the nerves that exit the spinal cord and on the muscles surrounding the vertebral column. This pressure leads to clinical signs of pain and marked hind end weakness. Because it can be easily mistaken for hip dysplasia or arthritis, radiographs (X rays) are needed to confirm a diagnosis.

Treatment: Affected dogs can be treated with anti-inflammatory medications to decrease the pain associated with the condition, but unfortunately, there is no definitive cure.

✔ Gingival hyperplasia: Enlarged, rounded gums that often grow over the tooth surfaces characterize gingival hyperplasia. Mouth pain, periodontal disease, and a diminished appetite often accompany this disorder.

Treatment: Application of medications directly to the gums, or, in severe instances, surgical removal of the excess gum tissue.

✔ Cryptorchidism: Both testicles or testes should be present in the scrotum of a puppy by six to ten months of age. Some breeds, among them the Boxer, show an increased incidence of the condition known as cryptorchidism, when one or both testicles fail to descend to the scrotum. It is important that a male dog has two fully descended testes. If this is not the case, such a dog is called a "cryptorchid."

The testes inside an unborn puppy are attached to the scrotum by a ligament that contracts after the birth of the animal, causing the testicles to descend through the so-called inguinal canal into the scrotum. This process takes about two weeks, and after that time the testes can often be felt. However, as the puppy grows, fat in the scrotum often makes it difficult to feel the testes for a while, but this changes again after approximately four months.

Cryptorchids should obviously never be used for breeding, as cryptorchidism may be inherited by the offspring, although an implant of testosterone could help the male dog.

Treatment: The veterinarian will remove the retained testis surgically. Retained testicles are prone to cancer.

General First Aid

If you suspect the presence of a disease, first check to see whether your Boxer has fever or possibly a subnormal temperature. If your pet's temperature is below or above the normal range of 100.4 to 102.5°F (38–39.2°C), it may be ill.

Taking the Dog's Temperature

The generally accepted opinion that if a Boxer's nose is hot it has fever is incorrect. The body temperature of a Boxer can be safely and reliably determined only by measuring it with a digital thermometer. It is a good idea to have someone help you perform the procedure. One person should hold the dog's head and speak to it soothingly while the other carefully inserts the thermometer into the rectum and holds it there until the reading is obtained. Lubricate the tip of the thermometer with some petroleum jelly beforehand.

Administering Medicine

Tablets can be given to your Boxer by concealing them in some liverwurst or ground

Some of the items in a first-aid kit: gauze pads, tweezers, antibiotic ointment, and surgical tape. Consult your veterinarian for more information.

beef. Some animals, however, then refuse to touch the food at all—even if the tablets are pulverized.

Tip: If that happens, open your Boxer's mouth and push the tablet as far back into its throat as possible. Then hold its jaws shut until it has swallowed the medication.

Liquid medications are best given to your Boxer with a disposable syringe, without the needle. Such syringes are available in pharmacies. Hold your Boxer's head up, insert the syringe at one side of the dog's mouth, and slowly let the liquid trickle between its lip and teeth.

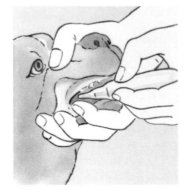

Let liquid medication trickle into the dog's mouth from one side.

Giving new meaning to the term "puppy dog eyes."

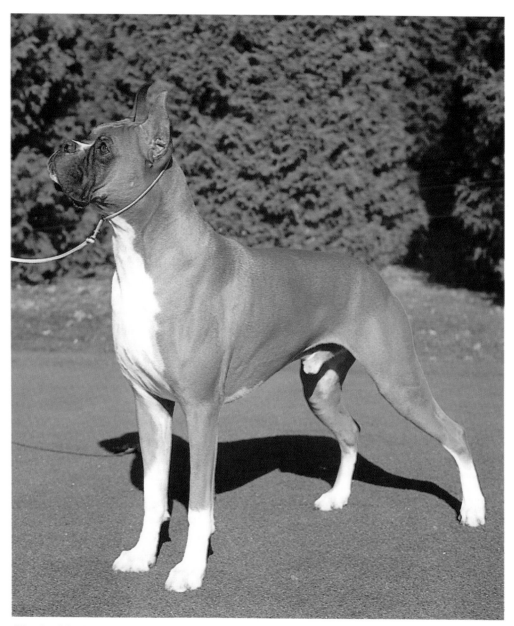

This healthy Boxer seems ready for the dog show.

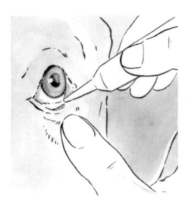

Left: Place eye ointment on the inside of the lower lid.

Right: An Elizabethan collar will keep the boxer from removing bandages.

Powder: With the tip of your finger, place it on your pet's tongue or on the inside of its lip.

Suppositories have to be lubricated with some petroleum jelly before insertion. Push them as deeply as possible into the dog's rectum. You can wear a plastic glove for this procedure.

Eye ointment and eyedrops should be placed inside the lower lid. To do so, pull the eyelid slightly downward.

Cardiopulmonary Resuscitation (CPR)

Prior to performing CPR on your Boxer, you must determine whether or not your pet has stopped breathing and if it has, whether or not its heart is beating. As a result, begin by observing the chest closely for breathing or noticeable movement. If none are seen within 20 seconds, artificial respiration will be needed.

Check the status of your dog's heartbeat by placing your hand on the bottom of your dog's chest (just behind the elbows) and press in to feel for a heartbeat. You can also check for a pulse by 1) placing your finger in the furrow on the neck on either side of its windpipe, or 2) pressing your fingers on the middle inside portion of the hind leg near its junction with the body. If no pulse is detected, you must institute external heart massage in conjunction with the artificial respiration.

Clear the mouth of any foreign objects or debris with your finger, then pull the tongue straight out towards you, closing your dog's mouth once you have done so. Next, put your mouth over your pet's nose and blow into the nostrils. Now release your mouth, letting your dog exhale. You will want to repeat this sequence every five seconds until your dog is breathing on its own or until you can obtain veterinary help.

If external heart massage is needed, position your dog on its right side. With the heel of one hand covering the front third of the rib cage (just behind the point of the elbow) and the other hand placed on top of the first, compress the chest inwards using a firm, smooth motion, then release immediately. Repeat these compressions at the rate of one or two per second. After every five compressions, perform another artificial respiration. Continue this procedure until you can get your Boxer to your veterinarian. Be sure to check for pulse or heartbeat frequently, and if detected, discontinue any further external heart massage.

Dressing Wounds

Minor injuries: The dog will clean these itself by licking them, but you should keep an eye on these kinds of injuries as well, to ensure that no serious infection develops.

Profusely bleeding wounds have to be bandaged with a pressure dressing. First, using tweezers, try to remove all foreign bodies from the wound. Next, fold a piece of clean cloth to make a thick pad and press it against the bleeding wound. Then tie a scarf or a thin bandage around the affected part of the body.

Important: Heavily bleeding wounds on the legs require a second bandage, a tourniquet tied above the site of the injury. Loosen this bandage from time to time, however, to allow blood to circulate in the leg. See the veterinarian immediately.

Wounds that are healing cause itching, and the Boxer tries to deal with the problem by gnawing and biting at the spot. Ask your veterinarian how you can help your pet if that happens. The Boxer also instinctively tries to remove bandages in order to lick its wounds. You need to prevent that by putting an Elizabethan collar on your pet.

Remedies for Insect Stings

The sting of a bee or a wasp, especially in the throat area, can place your Boxer in mortal danger. Severe swellings in that area lead to difficulty in breathing and swallowing. Allergic reactions that cause circulatory disturbances are possible as well, however.

What to do: With every type of sting, the first step is to get your Boxer calmed down. If it is a bee sting, remove the stinger if possible. Unusual reactions to a bee sting always require a trip to the veterinarian. Instant treatment by a veterinarian is absolutely imperative if a bee or a wasp has stung your Boxer in the throat area. If it has been stung on the lip or some other body part or parts, cool down the affected area with cold compresses.

Poisoning

The first symptoms of poisoning are severe vomiting, diarrhea, convulsions, circulatory collapse, labored breathing, severe irritation of the mucous membranes in the eye and throat areas, and possible blue coloration of the tongue.

What to do: Everything that is poisonous to your Boxer should be kept out of its reach. If, despite all your precautions, your pet has ingested poisonous substances, take it to the veterinarian without delay.

Heatstroke

Boxers most commonly are affected by heatstroke, especially when they are old or fat, when left behind in a parked car in the broiling sun. Heatstroke also can occur in rooms without adequate ventilation or when the dog has physically overtaxed itself. These are the results:

✔ circulatory collapse
✔ weakness
✔ heavy panting accompanied by excessive drooling and a staring expression
✔ fast-pounding pulse
✔ rise in body temperature (over 106°F [41°C])

What to do: If these symptoms appear, place damp cloths around your Boxer's body; they are most effective in the head area. Carry the dog into the shade. Take its body temperature. The dog has to be examined by a veterinarian, even if its condition has improved.

A Boxer pup striking a regal pose.

In summer, it's imperative to keep an eye out for signs of heatstroke.

✔ **Proptosed globe** (eyeball bulges out of its socket) commonly occurs in all so-called brachycephalic dog breeds, like Pugs and Boxers. Immediate veterinary care is essential. If the eyeball remains exposed for a long period of time, the cornea will dry out and it may be impossible for the veterinarian to save the eye.

Treatment (first aid): Apply ophthalmic eyewash to keep the cornea moist at all times. Don't use tap water or anything that is not the right osmotic concentration. As soon as possible, get to the veterinarian, who will quickly replace the eyeball in the socket.

Transportation to the Veterinarian

If you transport your Boxer to the veterinarian's office in a car, you should have a dog carrier in the vehicle. This is the safest alternative for both the dog and the driver. However, in the absence of such a carrier, it is wise to have another person ride with you. During the trip, your companion can look after the dog in the back seat and make every effort to keep it calm. If the Boxer is seriously injured, contact the veterinarian before bringing in your pet. He or she will tell you the best way to transport the dog.

Taking in two Boxers is a huge responsibility, but it can be twice as rewarding!

It is a good idea to give an at-home health exam once a month. Designed to supplement routine veterinary checkups, these exams can be useful in detecting diseases and disorders in their early stages.

Step 1: Evaluate Your Boxer's General Appearance

Start by taking a step back and observing your Boxer. Watch how it moves. Is there an abnormality in its gait? An abnormal gait with or without limping or lameness could indicate weakness or a disturbance in either the nervous system or musculoskeletal system. Dogs experiencing lameness will often dip their head as they walk. Injuries, arthritis, spondylosis, and tumors can cause lameness.

How is your Boxer's posture? Postures characterized by a wide-based stance with the neck extended indicate breathing difficulties, usually caused by heart or lung disease. An arched back accompanied by a reluctance to move is often indicative of abdominal pain. Note the position of your dog's head. Boxers that shake or tilt their heads often have an ear disorder.

Assess your pet's overall attitude. Is it alert and active, or has it been more withdrawn, lethargic or irritable?

As you might expect, sick or injured animals often display such attitudes.

Step 2: Check Pulse, Respiratory Rate, Temperature, and Body Weight

Take your Boxer's pulse by gently pressing your fingers against the upper, inner portion of a leg. Normal resting pulse for a Boxer can range from 60 to 120 beats per minute. An abnormal pulse that accompanies other clinical signs of disease should be reported to your veterinarian immediately. Count how many breaths your Boxer takes within a minute's time. This should be anywhere from 12 to 15, depending upon your dog's activity level. Rapid respiration should prompt you to contact your veterinarian.

Next, take your dog's temperature using a digital thermometer. The normal body temperature for Boxers ranges from 99.5 to 102.2°F. Excited pets may have elevated temperatures, but even then it should rarely exceed 103.5°F.

After obtaining temperature, pulse, and respiration readings, weigh your dog. Unexplained or consistent weight loss or weight gain should prompt you to contact your veterinarian. Parasitism,

intestinal disturbances, and cancer can cause significant weight loss. On the flipside, pampered Boxers have been known to become obese. An overweight Boxer needs to be put on a diet and an exercise program formulated and prescribed by its veterinarian.

Step 3: Closer Evaluation

Approach the remaining portion of your health check systematically, starting at the head and working back.

Eyes: Check your Boxer's eyes for redness, cloudiness, discharge, squinting or unequal pupil size. The presence of one or more of these signs could indicate infection, trauma, glaucoma, or ulcers. A red or yellow tinge to the white portion of the eyeball could indicate inflammation or jaundice, respectively. A thorough exam by a veterinarian is the only way to determine the true cause of an eye disorder.

Eyelids: Be sure that no foreign objects, eyelashes, or hairs are irritating the surfaces of the eyes. Constant, untreated irritation can lead to corneal injuries, which are extremely painful. Check for tumors or masses affecting the lids.

Ears: The ears should be clean and free of debris.

Check for any foul smells or discharges. A black or brown discharge could signify an ear mite infestation or a yeast infection. A yellowish, creamy discharge usually means a bacterial infection or foreign body is present. Other signs of ear disease include scratching at the ears, and shaking or tilting the head.

Nose: The nose should be moist and free of discharges or ulcerations. Clear nasal discharges are caused by either allergies or viral infections. A green, mucoid discharge indicates bacterial infection, which can often occur secondarily to a foreign object lodged within the nose. Blood coming from the nose can result from trauma or tumors. Contrary to popular belief, a dry nose alone does not necessarily mean a dog is ill.

Mouth: Your Boxer's gums and mucous membranes should be moist and pink. Pale, dry mucous membranes may indicate anemia, dehydration, or shock. A capillary refill time should be obtained by pressing on the upper gum with your index finger, causing the region under your finger to turn white. Now remove your finger and see how long it takes for the gum to return to a pink color. If it takes longer than two seconds to do so, it may indicate a problem in your pet's circulation, and this warrants a call to your veterinarian. Further inspect the mouth for swollen gums, foreign objects, dental disease, tumors, and sores.

Skin and coat: Check your Boxer's skin and coat carefully for parasites, redness, oiliness, or infection. Is your dog itching or suffering from hair loss? Apart from fleas, this could be caused by food or pollen allergies, mange, ringworm, poor nutrition, or metabolic disorders.

Body: Feel over your Boxer's entire body for of any lumps or bumps. Take your time when doing this, as aging Boxers are highly prone to tumors. Lumps can also be abscesses, enlarged lymph nodes, granulomas, cysts, foreign bodies,

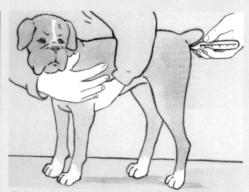

Taking the dog's temperature is a job for two people: One person holds the Boxer while the other inserts the thermometer.

or hernias). Always contact your dog's doctor if you detect an abnormal lump.

Gently press both sides of the abdomen just behind the ribcage and slowly work your way to the hip region. Note any obvious swelling, tenderness, or pain in this region. Look for any discharges involving the reproductive organs. Not all discharges are abnormal, but some indicate infection. If you feel or see anything strange, contact your veterinarian.

Tail region: Observe beneath the tail for any lesions, masses, or discharges. Look for tapeworm segments, which appear as tiny grains of rice. If you have noticed your dog scooting, continually biting at its rear end, or having difficulty defecating, it could have impacted anal sacs. Left untreated, impacted sacs can become infected and rupture.

Legs: Palpate each leg, noting any swollen or painful areas. Check the pressure points over the elbows, knees, and wrists for signs of hair loss or irritation. Finally, check the length of the nails. With your dog's paws planted squarely on the floor, the nails should barely touch the floor surface if at all.

BREEDING BOXERS

Breeding Boxers means steadily and continually improving the breed. If you decide to breed a female, or bitch, you have to be well acquainted with the breed characteristics and the breeding regulations (see The AKC Breed Standard, page 7). Moreover, you should belong to a breeders' club or association and adhere to their breeding regulations as well. An additional prerequisite for breeding is perfect health on the part of both breeding partners.

The right stud: In choosing the stud, not only its outward appearance—that is, its conformation—but also its temperament (see The AKC Breed Standard, page 7) is an important factor.

The Mating Act

Heat: The mating season begins with the estrual cycle of the bitch. A normally developed female first comes into season between her ninth and twelfth months of life. Every subsequent heat occurs at intervals of about seven months and lasts roughly 21 days. The minimum age at which a bitch may be bred is 18 months, according to the breeding regulations.

Readiness to mate: The heat begins with the swelling of the vagina and a bloody discharge. The bitch urinates more frequently and often does not squat so low during urination.

The Michael Jordan of Boxers, this little guy is an unbelievable jumper!

It is important to make a note of the day when the bloody discharge first appeared, because it is used to determine the period of time during which the bitch is willing to accept the attentions of a male. This phase begins on about the tenth day of the cycle and lasts six to seven days.

Mating act: Copulation usually is preceded by some preliminaries, typically including extensive sniffing of the sides of the neck and the ears. If that is followed by the actual mating act, both dogs remain "tied" together for some time. The tie may last 5 to 50 minutes.

Caution: During this phase, make no attempt to separate the animals, because wrenching them apart by force can result in serious injuries.

Tip: While in heat, a bitch absolutely has to be put on a leash when taken for a walk. The males follow the scent of a bitch in season and mate with her when they find her, if she happens to be at the right point of the estrual cycle. In addition, the bitch herself, in that stage of the cycle, will be on the lookout for a suitor, and she will not be exactly choosy about whom she selects.

Gestation

First and second weeks: In the first two weeks after her season has ended, a bitch, even if pregnant, shows scarcely any external signs. Many bitches, however, exhibit an increased need for sleep at the beginning of the gestation period. Nonetheless, they should continue to get sufficient exercise at this time.

Third and fourth weeks: After approximately three weeks, a pregnant bitch may possibly exhibit "morning sickness." That is no cause for concern, but merely a sign that her metabolism is adjusting to the changed conditions. It is also possible that she will eat somewhat more poorly at this time, and sometimes she will even lose a little weight.

Tip: Don't make the mistake of overfeeding your pet now. A slight weight loss in this situation is not a problem; excessive weight gain, however, is. The widespread view that a pregnant bitch has to eat more than usual is erroneous. Rather, she needs food of greater nutritive value, with a high energy content in particular.

Fifth to ninth weeks: In the fifth week of pregnancy, the bitch's girth begins to expand. She continues to need exercise, but the increased burden on her circulation and lungs has to be taken into account.

End of the gestation period: The normal gestation period of a Boxer bitch lasts between 61 and 63 days. Slightly longer or shorter gestations are completely within the realm of possibility, however. If a bitch carries longer than 65 days, the veterinarian should be consulted.

Size of the litter: The average size of a Boxer's litter is about seven puppies per whelping.

The Whelping Box

The bitch needs a whelping box for the delivery. It should be made of wood and measure at least 33 x 45 inches (84 x 114 cm). In addition, it has to be about 10 inches (25 cm)

high in front and roughly 20 to 24 inches (51–61 cm) high at the sides. To create the effect of a cave, cover the box with a blanket or a lid, but it's important that the covering you use be removable.

Guard rail: The interior of the box has to be provided with a guard rail. This strip of wood, about 3 to 4 inches (8–10 cm) thick, should be attached around the circumference of the entire box, about 6 inches (15 cm) from the bottom. It will keep the puppies from getting trapped or even squashed between the mother dog and the walls of the whelping box.

Furnishings: Various materials can be used to make a bed for the puppies. They include needled and stuffed felt and the so-called vet-drybed available commercially. For the whelping phase, you need to provide a moisture-proof pad, which you should cover well with absorbent paper.

The Whelping Process

The surest sign of impending labor is the dropping of the bitch's body temperature by 2.7 to 3.6°F. A Boxer's normal temperature usually is around 100°F (38°C). When whelping is imminent, the bitch becomes restless, starts to pant, and wants to urinate with great frequency. Often she also refuses to eat 12 to 24 hours before giving birth.

The whelping process itself begins with the premonitory pains, followed by the start of the final stage of labor, when the puppies are expelled. Each puppy is born in an amniotic sac with a placenta. The fetal membranes are torn open by the mother dog as she frees her offspring from the sac. The still-wet newborn triggers in its mother an impulse to lick. That stimulates not only the puppy's circulation, but also the activity of its digestive organs. The bitch consumes the sac and the placenta as she licks the puppy clean.

The Puppies' Development and Nutrition

First to third weeks of life: Shortly after birth, the puppies are defenseless, at the mercy of a host of pathogens. For this reason, their mother's milk is of enormous importance for the newborns. Along with it, a puppy ingests vital antibodies. In addition, this so-called colostrum also has a mildly laxative effect. The puppy drinks and immediately thereafter empties its bowel. The mother helps this process along by licking the puppy. As she does so, she consumes the waste matter, just as she did after the puppy was born.

The puppy's eyes remain closed for about the first 10 days, and the ears, for the first 12 days.

When the puppies reach three weeks of age, they should receive their first deworming treatment.

Fourth to seventh weeks: Roughly as the third week of life ends, the so-called imprinting phase begins (see Developmental Phases, page 41).

Important: At this time, it is essential to spend a lot of time playing with your puppies. It is through hand contact that they sense their special person and imprint on him or her.

Puppies' individual personality traits can be read from their behavior.

Eighth week of life: The most opportune time for the puppies to go to new homes is two months after their birth, at the beginning of the socialization phase (see Developmental Phases, page 41).

Pointer: Before being handed over to their buyers, the puppies first should have been wormed a second time and given their first series of vaccinations (see What the Buyer Needs to Know, page 15).

Weight check: The daily weighing of the puppies should be a matter of course for you. In this way you can immediately detect developmental disturbances in individual animals, because they can be read from insufficient weight gain. If the entire litter is not gaining weight normally, however, the fault lies with the mother dog. If she has no organic defects, you, as the breeder, have to give the puppies extra food in this case. Sometimes that may be necessary as early as the third week after birth.

Showing Your Boxer

Dog shows are conformation shows that give an overview of the current state of breeding programs. They usually are held outdoors in an area designated as the "ring." The individual

Your Boxer will eventually become a very important part of your family—some even take up tennis and driving a car!

Boxers, in various age groupings and in accordance with their level of specialized training, are judged separately, according to sex and color, by conformation judges (see The AKC Breed Standard, page 7). The best of their class are awarded prizes, and their owners receive a certificate attesting to that fact.

Prerequisite: Participation in national as well as international conformation shows is open only to registered Boxers. "Registered" means that your Boxer is listed in the records of the American Kennel Club and often of the appropriate Boxer club, which contain the breed lines of its ancestors as well as those of Boxers, for many decades, back to the beginning of the Boxer breed (see Information, page 92). A certain level of discipline and good training on the part of your Boxer are required for appropriate showmanship. For example, you have to be able to show the conformation judge your dog's teeth. Leash training and obedience are equally indispensable. Without them, even judging the dog's gait is impossible. Boxers that react aggressively to every other dog or possibly even to humans will never excel in the ring. Only a good-tempered, beautiful dog that stands out from its competitors by virtue of its impressive behavior can captivate the judges. With head proudly lifted, it will raise itself to its full height to make as imposing an appearance as possible. Incidentally, every naturally talented Boxer will display such behavior in the show ring.

But regardless of how many points your Boxer earns at the show, for you, your dog should always be the best and most beautiful.

The Do's and Don'ts of Dog Ownership

Now that you have a firm grasp on what it takes to properly care for a Boxer, let's end with a list of basics that every dog owner should know:

DO:

✔ Respect your pet and his right to rest, peace, and privacy.

✔ Allow him the basic needs for healthy and nourishing food, plenty of clean, fresh water, his own toys, and a comfortable place to sleep.

✔ Protect him from harm, including teasing, harassment, or abuse from people who don't appreciate the special relationship one can develop with a pet.

✔ Learn the danger signals when meeting other dogs for the first time so you avoid misunderstanding, fright, and possible injury.

✔ Be aware of your dog's body language and eye expressions so you can easily detect when he is not feeling well or something is wrong.

DON'T:

✔ Disturb your dog when he is eating or sleeping.

✔ Carry a lot of food around the house. This can be very distracting and unfair to the dog who is on a feeding schedule.

✔ Put your face next to a dog's face suddenly—this will startle him, and especially if the dog doesn't know you, it can result in a bite caused by fear.

✔ Stare at your dog long and intensely. This may be seen as a challenge or provocation and could result in trouble.

✔ Have children screaming and racing around your dog—this could cause hysteria and result in nipping or biting.

✔ Exercise a strong dog, like a Boxer, without an adult to help in case he gets too hard to control.

✔ Poke, grab, pull ears or tail, step on paws, ride or throw yourself on a dog, especially when he is eating or sleeping.

✔ Try to stop a fight between dogs, whether they are your own or not.

✔ Touch a strange dog, whether loose or on a leash, without permission.

Kennel Clubs

American Kennel Club
51 Madison Avenue
New York, NY 10038
www.akc.org

Canadian Kennel Club
Commerce Park
89 Skyway Ave., Suite 100
Etobicoke, Ontario
 Canada M9W 6R4

American Boxer Club*
6310 Edward Drive
Clinton, MD 20735-4135
www.akc.org/clubs/abc/abc-home.htm

American Boarding Kennel Association
4575 Galley Road, Suite 400A
Colorado Springs, CO 80915
(publishes lists of approved
 boarding kennels)

American Society for the Prevention
 of Cruelty to Animals (ASPCA)
441 East 92nd Street
New York, NY 10128
www.aspca.org

American Veterinary Medical Association
930 North Meacham Road
Schaumburg, IL 60173
www.avma.org

Humane Society of the United States (HSUS)
2100 L Street NW
Washington, DC 20037
www.hsus.org

Books

 In addition to the most recent edition
of the official publication of the American
Kennel Club, *The Complete Dog Book*, other
suggestions include:

Coile, Caroline D. et al. *Barron's Encyclopedia
 of Dog Breeds.* Hauppauge, NY: Barron's
 Educational Series, Inc., 1998.

____. *Show Me! A Dog Showing Primer.* Haup-
 pauge, NY: Barron's Educational Series, Inc.,
 1997.

Dennis, Helen. *101 Questions Your Dog Would
 Ask: What's Bothering Your Dog and How to
 Solve Its Problems.* Hauppauge, NY: Barron's
 Educational Series, Inc., 1999.

Harper, Don. *The Dog Owner's Question and
 Answer Book.* Hauppauge, NY: Barron's
 Educational Series, Inc., 1998.

O'Brien, Jacqui. *Train Your Dog: A Weekly
 Program for a Well-Behaved Dog.* Hauppauge,
 NY: Barron's Educational Series, Inc., 1999.

Pinney, Chris. *Caring for Your Older Dog.* Hauppauge, NY: Barron's Educational Series, Inc.,
 1996.

Note: These addresses may change as new
officers are elected. The latest listing can
always be obtained from the American
Kennel Club.

Who could resist paying health insurance premiums for these two pretty faces?

Health Insurance for Dogs

Veterinary Pet Insurance, Inc.	*www.veterinarypetinsurance.com*
Preferred PetHealth Plus	*www.pethealthplus.com*
Petshealth Insurance	*www.petshealthinsurance.com*
PetAssure	*www.petassure.com*

About the Author

Johanna Thiel has been a Boxer owner for more than two decades. Since 1980 she has bred Boxers under the kennel name "vom Breuleck," and since 1989 she has been a breeding supervisor in the Frankfurt/Main Group of the Boxer Club. Together with her husband, who is a teacher-trainer in the same organization, she has had a long series of extraordinary successes in breeding Boxers.

Photo Credits

Norvia Behling: 68, 72 (top l/bottom l); Tara Darling: 21 bottom), 37 (bottom rr), 49 (bottom l/r), 56 (top r), 77, 88 (top l), 89 (top l/middle l); Tracy Hendrickson: 12, 16 (l), 36, 44 (r), 60, 88 (bottom l/top r). Billy Hustace: 17, 21 (top l/r), 37 (top l), 40, 45 (top), 48 (bottom l), 52, 56 (top l), 64 (top), 65 (bottom), 72 (top r/bottom r), 80 (r), 84; Curtis Hustace: 4, 8, 24, 32, 88 (bottom r), 89 (top r/bottom r); Pets by Paulette: 3, 16 (r), 20, 28 (bottom l/r), 37 (top r/bottom l), 45 (bottom), 48 (bottom r), 76, 80, 81; Christine Steimer: 28 (top), 29 (top), 44 (l), 48 (top), 49 (top), 57, 64 (bottom), 65 (top), 73 (bottom); Jean Wentworth: 9, 29 (bottom), 56 (bottom), 89 (bottom l), 93.

Cover Photos

Front: Billy Hustace; Inside front: Jean Wentworth; Inside back: Tara Darling; Back: Pets by Paulette.

Important Note

This pet owner's manual tells the reader how to buy and care for a Boxer. The advice given in this book is meant primarily for normally developed puppies from a good breeder, dogs of excellent physical health and good character traits.

Anyone who adopts a fully grown dog should be aware that the animal has already formed its basic impressions of human beings. The new owner should observe the dog very carefully, including its behavior toward humans, and should meet the previous owner. If the dog comes from an animal shelter, it may be possible to get some information on the dog's background and characteristics.

In addition, make sure your dog gets all the necessary immunizations and is wormed periodically (see page 69); otherwise, the health of humans and animals alike is placed at risk. If your dog shows signs of illness, it is essential to consult a veterinarian. If you have questions about your own health, see your physician and tell him or her that you keep a dog.

A Word about Pronouns

Many Boxer lovers (including this one) feel that the pronoun "it" is not appropriate when referring to a pet that can be such a wonderful part of our lives. However, for solely editorial reasons, we have used "it" in situations where the text refers to either a male or female Boxer. This was done simply to avoid the clumsiness of "he or she" in many places, and is in no way meant to lessen the value of animals in the world.

All inquiries should be addressed to:
Barron's Educational Series, Inc.
250 Wireless Boulevard
Hauppauge, NY 11788
http://www.barronseduc.com

International Standard Book No. 0-7641-1051-9

Library of Congress Catalog Card No. 00-030359

Library of Congress Cataloging-in-Publication Data
Thiel, Johanna.
    [Boxer. English]
    Boxers / Johanna Thiel.
        p. cm.
    ISBN 0-7641-1051-9
    1. Boxer (Dog breed). I. Title.
SF429.B75 T4813   2000
636.73—dc21   00-030359

Printed in Hong Kong

9 8 7 6 5 4 3 2 1